Oliver Goldsmith

She Stoops to Conquer

Or, The Mistakes of a Night

A COMEDY

EDITED BY

HAROLD LITTLEDALE

M.A., Litt.D.(Dublin)

Professor of English Language and Literature
University College of South Wales, Cardiff

BLACKIE & SON LIMITED
LONDON AND GLASGOW

BLACKIE & SON LIMITED
66 Chandos Place, London
17 Stanhope Street, Glasgow

BLACKIE & SON (INDIA) LIMITED
103/5 Fort Street, Bombay

BLACKIE & SON (CANADA) LIMITED
Toronto

BOOK
PRODUCTION
WAR ECONOMY
STANDARD

Printed in Great Britain by Blackie & Son, Ltd., Glasgow

INTRODUCTION.

GOLDSMITH'S first play, the *Good-natured Man* (1768), met with only moderate success on the stage, but it brought him about £400 for three "author's nights," and £100 for the copyright when it was published; a larger and more easily earned sum than he could have gained by any other kind of literary work. Poetry brought him reputation but not wealth. "I cannot afford," he said to Lord Lisburn, "to court the draggletail muses, my Lord, they would let me starve; but by my other labours I can make shift to eat, and drink, and have good clothes" (Forster, p. 352). So he worked away at paying compilations, such as his *History of Animated Nature*, and began (in 1771) to sketch a second comedy, on "the mistakes of a night."

It is said that the groundwork of this play was suggested to him by an adventure which had befallen himself in 1744, when he was returning to Mr. Hughes' school at Edgeworthstown, after spending his holidays at Lissoy. His sister, Catherine Hodson, has left us an account of the episode, which will be found quoted in the Introduction to Routledge's edition of Goldsmith's *Works;* but Mr. Forster (*Life of Goldsmith*, p. 14) gives a livelier and more detailed narrative of the affair. He says: "At the close of his last holidays, then a lad of nearly seventeen, he left home for Edgeworthstown, mounted on a borrowed hack which a friend was to restore to Lissoy, and with store of unaccustomed wealth, a guinea, in his pocket. The delicious taste of independence beguiled him to a loitering, lingering, pleasant enjoyment of the journey; and, instead of finding himself under Mr. Hughes' roof at nightfall, night fell upon him some two or three miles out of the direct road, in the middle of the streets of Ardagh. But nothing could disconcert the owner of the guinea, who, with a lofty, confident air, inquired of a person passing the way to the town's best house of entertainment. The man addressed was the wag of Ardagh, a humorous fencing-master, Mr. Cornelius Kelly, and the school-boy swagger was irresistible provocation to a jest. Submissively he turned back with horse and rider till they came within a pace or two of the great Squire Featherston's, to which he respectfully pointed as the 'best house' of Ardagh. Oliver rang at the gate, gave his beast in charge with authoritative rigour, and was shown, as a supposed expected guest, into the comfortable parlour of the squire.

"Those were days when Irish inn-keepers and Irish squires more nearly approximated than now; and Mr. Featherston, unlike the excellent but explosive Mr. Hardcastle, is said to have seen the mistake and

humoured it. Oliver had a supper which gave him so much satisfaction
that he ordered a bottle of wine to follow; and the attentive landlord
was not only forced to drink with him, but, with a like condescension,
the wife and pretty daughter were invited to the supper-room. Going
to bed, he stopped to give special instructions for a hot cake to break-
fast; and it was not till he had despatched this latter meal, and was
looking at his guinea with pathetic aspect of farewell, that the truth
was told him by the good-natured squire. The late Sir Thomas Featherston, grandson to the supposed innkeeper, had faith in the adventure;
and told Mr. Graham that as his grandfather and Charles Goldsmith
(Oliver's father) had been college acquaintances, it might be the better
accounted for."

The story may be true, but the existence of similar anecdotes in connection with other celebrated men or works, for instance the story of
Lady Alice Egerton in the Ludlow woods as a groundwork for *Comus*,
should make us cautious of giving it too ready belief. It is, however,
highly probable, and, true or not, very characteristic of Oliver Goldsmith, boy and man.

The new play, begun in 1771, was finished in 1772, and, in fulfilment
of an old promise, offered to George Colman, the manager of Covent
Garden Theatre, where *The Good-natured Man* had also been brought
out. The coolness between Goldsmith and Garrick, which had arisen
over Garrick's criticisms on the character of Lofty, and other points
in *The Good-natured Man*, had now come to an end; and it is tolerably
certain that but for his promise to Colman, Goldsmith would have first
offered the play to his friend Garrick at Drury Lane, and that Garrick
would have accepted it. And Colman would seem to have not appre-
ciated the excellence of the comedy when it was laid before him. He
kept it by him for some months, and evaded giving the impatient
author a decisive answer. At last Goldsmith became more urgent, and
in the middle of January, 1773, wrote to Colman *entreating* him to
relieve him from the state of suspense in which he had been kept for
so long. Whatever objections Colman might have he would endeavour
to remove, and not argue about them. He refused to allow the play to
be submitted to any other judgment than Colman's own, and hoped
that Colman would not treat him as badly as Garrick had once done,
in referring his first play to a committee. He concluded as follows:—
"I have, as you know, a large sum of money to make up shortly; by
accepting my play I can readily satisfy my creditor that way, at any
rate I must look about to some certainty to be prepared. For God's
sake take the play and let us make the best of it, and let me have the
same measure at least which you have given as bad plays as mine."

Colman's reply was to send back the manuscript, with various "dis-
tasteful remarks written in upon the blank leaves," but with a renewal
of his promise to produce the piece nevertheless. In his first resentment at Colman's remarks, Goldsmith hastily offered the play to
Garrick, and then, by Johnson's advice, as hastily retracted his offer.

Johnson's advice, "the advice of a sensible friend," as Goldsmith called it in his letter of recall, would seem to have been that it would be disadvantageous to withdraw in a marked manner from Covent Garden; and Johnson had an interview with Colman, "who was prevailed on at last by much solicitation, nay, a kind of force," to determine on the production of the play (Forster, p. 412).

What strikes us as most curious in all this is that Colman should have been so totally insensible to the spirit and humour of the play as first to hesitate about its acceptance and subsequently to predict its certain failure.   Some of the best actors took Colman's view of the play's prospects, and refused to act in it; but their places were supplied by others, and the rehearsals proceeded. A few days before the performance the task of choosing a catching name for the new piece was undertaken. " 'We are all in labour,' says Johnson, whose labour of kindness had been untiring throughout, 'for a name to Goldy's play.' What now stands as the second title, *The Mistakes of a Night*, was originally the only one; but it was thought undignified for a comedy. *The Old House a New Inn* was suggested in place of it, but dismissed as awkward. Reynolds then announced what he thought so capital a title, that he threatened, if it were not adopted, he should go and help to damn the play; and he triumphantly named it *The Belle's Stratagem*. This name was still under discussion, and had well-nigh been snatched from Mrs. Cowley, when Goldsmith, in whose ears, perhaps, Dryden's line may have lingered,

'But kneels to conquer, and but stoops to rise,'

hit upon *She Stoops to Conquer*." (F. p. 415).

The eventful night, March 15th, 1773, arrived at length, and the play, contrary to very general expectation, proved a brilliant triumph for its author.

The verdict of that first-night audience has many times been confirmed since, and *She Stoops to Conquer* still holds the highest place among eighteenth century comedies in the estimation of modern playgoers.

It has often been (rather unprofitably) debated whether this play is really a comedy or (as Horace Walpole said) only a farce,[1] but such a question could only have arisen upon a very limited conception of the true nature of a comedy, and a very exaggerated notion of the proper province of a farce. In the eighteenth century the term *comedy* had come to be applied chiefly to the comedy of manners and sentiments; but the older forms of comedy, depending for their interest upon romantic elements, or on characters and " humours," or on situations and incidents, were not less truly comedies in the proper comprehension of the term. A *farce*, originally the profane or immoral *farsa* of the Italian theatre, had in England come to mean a broadly comic interlude, or short play containing grotesque and undignified situations. In this sense a farce may be regarded as a subdivision of the comedy

[1] See Black's *Life of Goldsmith*, "Eng. Men of Letters," p. 145.

of incident. It is this relationship to comedy which has led to the
question being raised about our play; for it must be admitted that the
essential humour of the piece depends less upon the sparkling dialogue
and the quaint delineation of character, rich though these elements are,
than upon the ludicrous incongruity of the situations; it turns on "the
mistakes," not "the mistake" of a night—the perpetration of blunder
after blunder by the characters, while the audience are in the secret of
the true situation all the time. But on the other hand the plot is too
elaborate, the characterization too strongly marked, for us to regard the
play as other than a pure comedy, full of character, incident, and wit,
the main elements of the different schools of comedy blended and har-
monized into one; not as a comedy degenerating into farce, but rather
as occasionally refining and elevating farcical episodes to the level of the
highest comedy.

In his method of drawing character, and in the type of characters he
drew, Goldsmith took as his model George Farquhar (1678-1707), an
Irish dramatist who flourished during the reigns of William III. and
Anne; but he far outwent his model. In style, in humour, in purity
of thought, in dramatic power, there can be no comparison between
the two men; and the point is only interesting because Goldsmith has
himself suggested it, and because inquiry lets us see how little he has
really taken. A few isolated expressions can here and there be detected
which may owe a hint to Farquhar. For instance, Oriana's saying
"who can be miser in another's wealth that is prodigal of his own"
(Farquhar, *The Inconstant*, iv. 2), may have suggested Miss Richland's
reply to Honeywood: "I see that it is in vain to expect happiness from
him, who has been so bad an economist of his own;" an expression that
is also found in the *Vicar of Wakefield*, chap. xiii. Again, the general
idea of young Marlow's character, "the bashful man," is a commonplace
of the stage, but some suggestion of it may have been found in Farquhar's character of Capt. Duretête in *The Inconstant.* As in act I.:—

"*Duretête.*—Ay, Mirabel, you will do well enough, but what will become of
your friend? you know I am so plaguy bashful, so naturally an ass upon these
occasions, that—" &c.

Or in act II., when Mirabel is leaving him with the lady, as Hastings
leaves young Marlow:—

"*Dur.*—Hold! hold! Why, Mirabel, friend, sure you won't be so barbarous
as to leave me alone! Prithee speak to her for yourself, as it were," &c.

But the very slightness of these similarities is sufficient to indicate
the degree of Goldsmith's obligations to Farquhar or anyone else. The
hearty country household at "the Old Buck's Head on the hill" are all
of his own creation. In the character of old Hardcastle, Goldsmith
drew a full-length portrait of the "fine old English gentleman, all of
the olden time," with his love for everything that's old: "old friends,
old times, old manners, old books, old wine," not omitting an "old

wife" who still affects to be young and fashionable. He has been a soldier, under the greatest military leader of his age (almost of any age), and veteran-like he loves to fight his battles over, and show "how fields were won," for the gratification of himself and the amazement of the country squires, his neighbours. We are given many indications of his real goodness of heart and simplicity of nature. The familiarity of his servants, for instance, or his tolerance of his wife's whims, or of the pranks of that graceless cub Tony, show his kindness to all around him. Yet he is rather an imperious old gentleman, not very patient under contradiction; and the effect of young Marlow's patronage upon him, his effort to restrain himself for Sir Charles Marlow's sake when that old friend's bashful son orders him about, is intensely comic, and like all true humour, not without a touch of pathos in it.

Mrs. Hardcastle, with all her weakness, has one element of strength, her love for her son, for whom she is ready to give her life (act V.), and whom she has spoiled through over-fondness. Here Goldsmith was upon familiar ground, for we have in her a reproduction, without essential differences, of the simple-minded though vain and illogical Mrs. Primrose. As Mrs. Primrose is deceived by the town splendours of Lady Blarney and Miss Wilhelmina Skeggs, so Mrs. Hardcastle is quite dazzled by Hastings' comments upon her air and manner, and his more than dubious compliment:—"I concluded you had been bred all your life either at Ranelagh, St. James', or Tower Wharf." As in the *Vicar of Wakefield*, so here, town and country manners are contrasted, and the innocent blunders of country people in aping the fashions and affectations of city people are held up for the ridicule of the town.

Of Miss Hardcastle and Miss Neville little need be said, although the former is the heroine, and gives its title to the play. The notion of adopting a disguise to win a lover is an old one, and had often done duty on the stage before Goldsmith adopted it; but it is a very attractive idea, and Miss Hardcastle, divested of her rank and fashionable dress, more truly " conquers" Marlow, and attracts our sympathies by her conquest, than would have been the case had she been plainly wooed and won like Miss Neville. The part of Miss Hardcastle was first played by Mrs. Bulkley (Miss Wilford), a very pretty actress, but one who unfortunately could not sing; and so the following little song, written for the part, had to be omitted (probably with some connecting dialogue) from the play :—

(AIR.—*The Humours of Ballymagairy.*)

Ah, me! when shall I marry me?
    Lovers are plenty ; but fail to relieve me.
He, fond youth, that could carry me,
    Offers to love, but means to deceive me.
But I will rally and combat the ruiner ;
    Not a look, not a smile, shall my passion discover.
She that gives all to the false one pursuing her,
    Makes but a penitent, and loses a lover.

Tony Lumpkin comes shouting on to the stage, and we never lose the ringing heartiness of that loud halloo throughout the play. His high spirits are infectious, and we feel inclined to admit his mother's excuses for him in part. After all, his is very unsophisticated wickedness; and then "the poor boy was always too sickly to do any good!" His name is well chosen, for Tony, short for Antony, was a cant name for a simpleton.[1] Yet Tony is no fool; he has plenty of low cunning, such as a spoiled child is apt to acquire if restricted in the means to indulge himself as he grows older. He has keys for all his mother's lock-ups; and it is he who hits on the plan for preventing Miss Neville from being safely *interned* in her Aunt Pedigree's fortress.

It will be remembered that the public cried out against *The Good-natured Man* for being low, and that after the first night the scene of the bailiffs had to be cut out in consequence. Goldsmith now took his revenge upon his critics by bringing their sentiments on the stage as those of the company at the *Three Jolly Pigeons*. Mr. Black (*Life of Goldsmith*, p. 143) well remarks: "Indeed, Goldsmith, however he might figure in society, was always capable of holding his own when he had his pen in his hand. And even at the outset of this comedy one sees how much he has gained in literary confidence since the writing of *The Good-natured Man*. Here there is no anxious stiffness at all; but a brisk, free conversation, full of point that is not too formal, and yet conveying all the information that has usually to be crammed into a first scene. In taking as his groundwork that old adventure that had befallen himself—his mistaking a squire's house for an inn—he was hampering himself with something that was not the less improbable because it had actually happened; but we begin to forget all the im-probabilities through the naturalness of the people to whom we are introduced, and the brisk movement and life of the piece."

It is not known how much money Goldsmith received for this play; but it cannot have been less, and probably was more, than he obtained by his first and less successful venture.

Postscript.—Since writing the foregoing I have noted the following in Prof. Ward's *Eng. Dramatic Literature*, ii. 596: — Farquhar's *Beaux' Stratagem* "is written in the happiest of veins; and may be regarded as the prototype of Goldsmith's *She Stoops to Conquer*, like which it hovers rather doubtfully on the borders—not always easy to determine —between comedy and farce."

----

[1] See Dryden, Globe Edition, p. 433.

SHE STOOPS TO CONQUER.

DEDICATION.

TO SAMUEL JOHNSON, LL.D.

DEAR SIR,—By inscribing this slight performance to you, I do not mean so much to compliment you as myself. It may do me some honour to inform the public, that I have lived many years in intimacy with you. It may serve the interests of mankind also to inform them, that the greatest wit may be found in a character, without impairing the most unaffected piety.

I have, particularly, reason to thank you for your partiality to this performance. The undertaking a comedy not merely sentimental was very dangerous; and Mr. Colman, who saw this piece in its various stages, always thought it so. However, I ventured to trust it to the public; and, though it was necessarily delayed till late in the season, I have every reason to be grateful.

I am, dear Sir, your most sincere friend and admirer,

OLIVER GOLDSMITH.

PROLOGUE.

BY DAVID GARRICK, ESQ.

Enter MR. WOODWARD, *dressed in black, and holding a handkerchief to his eyes.*

Excuse me, sirs, I pray—I can't yet speak—
I'm crying now—and have been all the week.
" 'Tis not alone this mourning suit," good masters:
" I've that within"—for which there are no plasters! (4)
Pray, would you know the reason why I'm crying?
The Comic Muse, long sick, is now a-dying!
And if she goes, my tears will never stop;
For as a player, I can't squeeze out one drop: (8)
I am undone, that's all—shall lose my bread—

9

I'd rather, but that's nothing—lose my head.
When the sweet maid is laid upon the bier,
Shuter and I shall be chief mourners here.   (12)
To her a mawkish drab of spurious breed,
Who deals in sentimentals, will succeed!
Poor Ned and I are dead to all intents;
We can as soon speak Greek as sentiments!   (16)
Both nervous grown, to keep our spirits up,
We now and then take down a hearty cup.
What shall we do?   If Comedy forsake us,
They'll turn us out, and no one else will take us.   (20)
But why can't I be moral?—Let me try—
My heart thus pressing—fixed my face and eye—
With a sententious look, that nothing means,
(Faces are blocks in sentimental scenes)   (24)
Thus I begin: "All is not gold that glitters,
"Pleasure seems sweet, but proves a glass of bitters.
"When Ignorance enters, Folly is at hand:
"Learning is better far than house and land.   (28)
"Let not your virtue trip; who trips may stumble,
"And virtue is not virtue, if she tumble."

I give it up—morals won't do for me;
To make you laugh, I must play tragedy.   (32)
One hope remains—hearing the maid was ill,
A Doctor comes this night to show his skill.
To cheer her heart, and give your muscles motion,
He, in Five Draughts prepar'd, presents a potion: (36)
A kind of magic charm—for be assur'd,
If you will swallow it, the maid is cur'd:
But desperate the Doctor, and her case is,
If you reject the dose, and make wry faces!   (40)
This truth he boasts, will boast it while he lives,
No poisonous drugs are mixed in what he gives.
Should he succeed, you'll give him his degree;
If not, within he will receive no fee!   (44)
The College *you*, must his pretensions back,
Pronounce him Regular, or dub him Quack.

DRAMATIS PERSONÆ.

SIR CHARLES MARLOW.
YOUNG MARLOW (his son).
HARDCASTLE.
HASTINGS.

TONY LUMPKIN.
DIGGORY.
MRS. HARDCASTLE.
MISS HARDCASTLE.

MISS NEVILLE.
MAID.
LANDLORD, SERVANTS, &c. &c.

ACT THE FIRST.

SCENE I.—*A Chamber in an old-fashioned House.*

Enter MRS. HARDCASTLE *and* MR. HARDCASTLE.

(1) *Mrs. Hard.* I vow, Mr. Hardcastle, you're very particular. Is there a creature in the whole country but ourselves, that does not take a trip to town now and then, to rub off the rust a little? There's the two Miss Hoggs, and our neighbour Mrs. Grigsby, go to take a month's polishing every winter.

(2) *Hard.* Ay, and bring back vanity and affectation to last them the whole year. I wonder why London cannot keep its own fools at home! In my time the follies of the town crept slowly among us, but now they travel faster than a stage-coach. Its fopperies come down not only as inside passengers, but in the very basket.

(3) *Mrs. Hard.* Ay, your times were fine times indeed; you have been telling us of them for many a long year. Here we live in an old rumbling mansion, that looks for all the world like an inn, but that we never see company. Our best visitors are old Mrs. Oddfish, the curate's wife, and little Cripplegate, the lame dancing-master; and all our entertainment your old stories of Prince Eugene and the Duke of Marlborough. I hate such old-fashioned trumpery.

(4) *Hard.* And I love it. I love everything that's old: old friends, old times, old manners, old books, old wine; and I believe, Dorothy (*taking her hand*), you'll own I have been pretty fond of an old wife.

(5) *Mrs. Hard.* Dear me, Mr. Hardcastle, you're for ever at your Dorothys and your old wifes. You may be a Darby, but I'll be no Joan, I promise you. I'm not so old as you'd make

me, by more than one good year. Add twenty to twenty, and make money of that.

(6) *Hard.* Let me see; twenty added to twenty makes just fifty and seven.

(7) *Mrs. Hard.* It's false, Mr. Hardcastle; I was but twenty when I was brought to bed of Tony, that I had by Mr. Lumpkin, my first husband; and he's not come to years of discretion yet.

(8) *Hard.* Nor ever will, I dare answer for him. Ay, you have taught him finely.

(9) *Mrs. Hard.* No matter. Tony Lumpkin has a good fortune. My son is not to live by his learning. I don't think a boy wants much learning to spend fifteen hundred a year.

(10) *Hard.* Learning, quotha! a mere composition of tricks and mischief.

(11) *Mrs. Hard.* Humour, my dear; nothing but humour. Come, Mr. Hardcastle, you must allow the boy a little humour.

(12) *Hard.* I'd sooner allow him a horse-pond. If burning the footmen's shoes, frightening the maids, and worrying the kittens be humour, he has it. It was but yesterday he fastened my wig to the back of my chair, and when I went to make a bow, I popt my bald head in Mrs. Frizzle's face.

(13) *Mrs. Hard.* And am I to blame? The poor boy was always too sickly to do any good. A school would be his death. When he comes to be a little stronger, who knows what a year or two's Latin may do for him.

(14) *Hard.* Latin for him! A cat and fiddle. No, no; the alehouse and the stable are the only schools he'll ever go to.

(15) *Mrs. Hard.* Well, we must not snub the poor boy now, for I believe we sha'n't have him long among us. Anybody that looks in his face may see he's consumptive.

(16) *Hard.* Ay, if growing too fat be one of the symptoms.

(17) *Mrs. Hard.* He coughs sometimes.

(18) *Hard.* Yes, when his liquor goes the wrong way.

(19) *Mrs. Hard.* I'm actually afraid of his lungs.

(20) *Hard.* And truly so am I; for he sometimes whoops like a speaking trumpet—(*Tony hallooing behind the scenes*)— O, there he goes—a very consumptive figure, truly.

Enter Tony, *crossing the stage.*

(21) *Mrs. Hard.* Tony, where are you going, my charmer! Won't you give papa and I a little of your company, lovee?

(22) *Tony.* I'm in haste, mother; I cannot stay.

(23) *Mrs. Hard.* You sha'n't venture out this raw evening, my dear; you look most shockingly.

(24) *Tony.* I can't stay, I tell you. The Three Pigeons expects me down every moment. There's some fun going forward.

(25) *Hard.* Ay; the alehouse, the old place: I thought so.

(26) *Mrs. Hard.* A low, paltry set of fellows.

(27) *Tony.* Not so low, neither. There's Dick Muggins the exciseman, Jack Slang the horse doctor, little Aminadab that grinds the music box, and Tom Twist that spins the pewter platter.

(28) *Mrs. Hard.* Pray, my dear, disappoint them for one night at least.

(29) *Tony.* As for disappointing them, I should not so much mind; but I can't abide to disappoint myself.

(30) *Mrs. Hard.* (*Detaining him.*) You sha'n't go.

(31) *Tony.* I will, I tell you.

(32) *Mrs. Hard.* I say you sha'n't.

(33) *Tony.* We'll see which is strongest, you or I.

[*Exit, hauling her out.*

(34) *Hard.* (*Solus.*) Ay, there goes a pair that only spoil each other, But is not the whole age in a combination to drive sense and discretion out of doors? There's my pretty darling Kate! the fashions of the times have almost infected her too. By living a year or two in town, she is as fond of gauze and French frippery as the best of them.

Enter Miss Hardcastle.

(35) *Hard.* Blessings on my pretty innocence! drest out as usual, my Kate. Goodness! What a quantity of superfluous silk hast thou got about thee, girl! I could never teach the fools of this age, that the indigent world could be clothed out of the trimmings of the vain.

(36) *Miss Hard.* You know our agreement, sir. You allow me the morning to receive and pay visits, and to dress in my own manner; and in the evening I put on my housewife's dress to please you.

(37) *Hard.* Well, remember, I insist on the terms of our agreement; and, by the bye, I believe I shall have occasion to try your obedience this very evening.

(38) *Miss Hard.* I protest, sir, I don't comprehend your meaning.

(39) *Hard.* Then to be plain with you, Kate, I expect the young gentleman I have chosen to be your husband from town this very day. I have his father's letter, in which he informs me his son is set out, and that he intends to follow himself shortly after.

(40) *Miss Hard.* Indeed! I wish I had known something of this before. Bless me, how shall I behave? It's a thousand to one I sha'n't like him; our meeting will be so formal, and so like a thing of business, that I shall find no room for friendship or esteem.

(41) *Hard.* Depend upon it, child, I'll never control your choice; but Mr. Marlow, whom I have pitched upon, is the son of my old friend, Sir Charles Marlow, of whom you have heard me talk so often. The young gentleman has been bred a scholar, and is designed for an employment in the service of his country. I am told he's a man of an excellent understanding.

(42) *Miss Hard.* Is he?

(43) *Hard.* Very generous.

(44) *Miss Hard.* I believe I shall like him.

(45) *Hard.* Young and brave.

(46) *Miss Hard.* I'm sure I shall like him.

(47) *Hard.* And very handsome.

(48) *Miss Hard.* My dear papa, say no more (*kissing his hand*), he's mine; I'll have him.

(49) *Hard.* And, to crown all, Kate, he's one of the most bashful and reserved young fellows in all the world.

(50) *Miss Hard.* Eh! you have frozen me to death again. That word *reserved* has undone all the rest of his accomplish-

ments. A reserved lover, it is said, always makes a suspicious husband.

(51) *Hard.* On the contrary, modesty seldom resides in a breast that is not enriched with nobler virtues. It was the very feature in his character that first struck me.

(52) *Miss Hard.* He must have more striking features to catch me, I promise you. However, if he be so young, so handsome, and so everything as you mention, I believe he'll do still. I think I'll have him.

(53) *Hard.* Ay, Kate, but there is still an obstacle. It's more than an even wager he may not have you.

(54) *Miss Hard.* My dear papa, why will you mortify one so? Well, if he refuses, instead of breaking my heart at his indifference, I'll only break my glass for its flattery, set my cap to some newer fashion, and look out for some less difficult admirer.

(55) *Hard.* Bravely resolved! In the mean time I'll go prepare the servants for his reception: as we seldom see company, they want as much training as a company of recruits the first day's muster.   [*Exit.*

(56) *Miss Hard.* (*Alone.*) Well, this news of papa's puts me all in a flutter. Young, handsome: these he put last; but I put them foremost. Sensible, good-natured; I like all that. But then reserved and sheepish; that's much against him. Yet can't he be cured of his timidity, by being taught to be proud of his wife? Yes, and can't I—But I vow I'm disposing of the husband before I have secured the lover.

Enter MISS NEVILLE.

(57) *Miss Hard.* I'm glad you're come, Neville, my dear. Tell me, Constance, how do I look this evening? Is there anything whimsical about me? Is it one of my well-looking days, child? Am I in face to-day?

(58) *Miss Nev.* Perfectly, my dear. Yet now I look again —bless me !—sure no accident has happened among the canary birds or the gold-fishes. Has your brother or the cat been meddling? or has the last novel been too moving?

(59) *Miss Hard.* No; nothing of all this. I have been

threatened—I can scarce get it out—I have been threatened with a lover.

(60) *Miss Nev.* And his name—

(61) *Miss Hard.* Is Marlow.

(62) *Miss Nev.* Indeed!

(63) *Miss Hard.* The son of Sir Charles Marlow.

(64) *Miss Nev.* As I live, the most intimate friend of Mr. Hastings, my admirer. They are never asunder. I believe you must have seen him when we lived in town.

(65) *Miss Hard.* Never.

(66) *Miss Nev.* He's a very singular character, I assure you. Among women of reputation and virtue he is the modestest man alive; but his acquaintance give him a very different character among creatures of another stamp: you understand me.

(67) *Miss Hard.* An odd character indeed. I shall never be able to manage him. What shall I do? Pshaw, think no more of him, but trust to occurrences for success. But how goes on your own affair, my dear? has my mother been courting you for my brother Tony as usual?

(68) *Miss Nev.* I have just come from one of our agreeable *tête-à-têtes.* She has been saying a hundred tender things, and setting off her pretty monster as the very pink of perfection.

(69) *Miss Hard.* And her partiality is such, that she actually thinks him so. A fortune like yours is no small temptation. Besides, as she has the sole management of it, I'm not surprised to see her unwilling to let it go out of the family.

(70) *Miss Nev.* A fortune like mine, which chiefly consists in jewels, is no such mighty temptation. But at any rate, if my dear Hastings be but constant, I make no doubt to be too hard for her at last. However, I let her suppose that I am in love with her son; and she never once dreams that my affections are fixed upon another.

(71) *Miss Hard.* My good brother holds out stoutly. I could almost love him for hating you so.

(72) *Miss Nev.* It is a good-natured creature at bottom, and I'm sure would wish to see me married to anybody but him-

self. But my aunt's bell rings for our afternoon's walk round the improvements. *Allons!* Courage is necessary, as our affairs are critical.

(73) *Miss Hard.* "Would it were bed-time, and all were well."   [*Exeunt.*

SCENE II.—*An Alehouse Room. Several shabby Fellows with punch and tobacco.* TONY *at the head of the table, a little higher than the rest, a mallet in his hand.*

(1) *Omnes.* Hurrea! hurrea! hurrea! bravo!

(2) *First Fel.* Now, gentlemen, silence for a song. The 'squire is going to knock himself down for a song.

(3) *Omnes.* Ay, a song, a song!

(4) *Tony.* Then I'll sing you, gentlemen, a song I made upon this alehouse, the Three Pigeons.

SONG.

Let schoolmasters puzzle their brain
    With grammar, and nonsense, and learning,
Good liquor, I stoutly maintain,
    Gives *genus* a better discerning.
Let them brag of their heathenish gods,
    Their Lethes, their Styxes, and Stygians,
Their Quis, and their Quæs, and their Quods,
    They're all but a parcel of Pigeons.
                Toroddle, toroddle, toroll.

When methodist preachers come down,
    A-preaching that drinking is sinful,
I'll wager the rascals a crown,
    They always preach best with a skinful.
But when you come down with your pence,
    For a slice of their scurvy religion,
I'll leave it to all men of sense,
    But you, my good friend, are the Pigeon.
                Toroddle, toroddle, toroll.

Then come, put the jorum about,
    And let us be merry and clever,
Our hearts and our liquors are stout,
    Here's the Three Jolly Pigeons for ever.
Let some cry up woodcock or hare,
    Your bustards, your ducks, and your widgeons;
But of all the *gay* birds in the air,
    Here's a health to the Three Jolly Pigeons.
                Toroddle, toroddle, toroll.

(5) *Omnes.* Bravo, bravo!

(6) *First Fel.* The 'squire has got spunk in him.

(7) *Second Fel.* I loves to hear him sing, bekeays he never gives us nothing that's low.

(8) *Third Fel.* O hang anything that's low, I cannot bear it.

(9) *Fourth Fel.* The genteel thing is the genteel thing any time: if so be that a gentleman bees in a concatenation accordingly.

(10) *Third Fel.* I likes the maxum of it, Master Muggins. What, though I am obligated to dance a bear, a man may be a gentleman for all that. May this be my poison, if my bear ever dances but to the very genteelest of tunes; "Water Parted," or "The minuet in Ariadne."

(11) *Second Fel.* What a pity it is the 'squire is not come to his own. It would be well for all the publicans within ten miles round of him.

(12) *Tony.* Faith, and so it would, Master Slang. I'd then show what it was to keep choice of company.

(13) *Second Fel.* O he takes after his own father for that. To be sure old 'Squire Lumpkin was the finest gentleman I ever set my eyes on. For winding the straight horn, or beating a thicket for a hare, or a wench, he never had his fellow. It was a saying in the place, that he kept the best horses, dogs, and girls, in the whole county.

(14) *Tony.* Faith, and when I'm of age, I'll be no bastard, I promise you. I have been thinking of Bet Bouncer and the miller's gray mare to begin with. But come, my boys, drink about and be merry, for you pay no reckoning. Well, Stingo, what's the matter?

Enter Landlord.

(15) *Land.* There be two gentlemen in a post-chaise at the door. They have lost their way upo' the forest; and they are talking something about Mr. Hardcastle.

(16) *Tony.* As sure as can be, one of them must be the gentleman that's coming down to court my sister. Do they seem to be Londoners?

(17) *Land.* I believe they may. They look woundily like Frenchmen.

(18) *Tony.* Then desire them to step this way, and I'll set them right in a twinkling. (*Exit* Landlord.) Gentlemen, as they mayn't be good enough company for you, step down for a moment, and I'll be with you in the squeezing of a lemon.

[*Exeunt mob.*

(19) *Tony.* (*Solus.*) Father-in-law has been calling me whelp and hound this half year. Now, if I pleased, I could be so revenged upon the old grumbletonian. But then I'm afraid —afraid of what? I shall soon be worth fifteen hundred a year, and let him frighten me out of *that* if he can.

Enter Landlord, *conducting* MARLOW *and* HASTINGS.

(20) *Mar.* What a tedious uncomfortable day have we had of it! We were told it was but forty miles across the country, and we have come above threescore.

(21) *Hast.* And all, Marlow, from that unaccountable reserve of yours, that would not let us inquire more frequently on the way.

(22) *Mar.* I own, Hastings, I am unwilling to lay myself under an obligation to every one I meet, and often stand the chance of an unmannerly answer.

(23) *Hast.* At present, however, we are not likely to receive any answer.

(24) *Tony.* No offence, gentlemen. But I'm told you have been inquiring for one Mr. Hardcastle in these parts. Do you know what part of the country you are in?

(25) *Hast.* Not in the least, sir, but should thank you for information.

(26) *Tony.* Nor the way you came?

(27) *Hast.* No, sir; but if you can inform us—

(28) *Tony.* Why, gentlemen, if you know neither the road you are going, nor where you are, nor the road you came, the first thing I have to inform you is, that—you have lost your way.

(29) *Mar.* We wanted no ghost to tell us that.

(30) *Tony.* Pray, gentlemen, may I be so bold so as to ask the place from whence you came?

(31) *Mar.* That's not necessary towards directing us where we are to go.

(32) *Tony.* No offence; but question for question is all fair, you know. Pray, gentlemen, is not this same Hardcastle a cross-grained, old-fashioned, whimiscal fellow, with an ugly face, a daughter, and a pretty son?

(33) *Hast.* We have not seen the gentleman; but he has the family you mention.

(34) *Tony.* The daughter, a tall, trapesing, trolloping, talk-ative maypole; the son, a pretty, well-bred, agreeable youth, that everybody is fond of.

(35) *Mar.* Our information differs in this. The daughter is said to be well-bred and beautiful; the son an awkward booby, reared up and spoiled at his mother's apron-string.

(36) *Tony.* He-he-hem!—Then, gentlemen, all I have to tell you is, that you won't reach Mr. Hardcastle's house this night, I believe.

(37) *Hast.* Unfortunate!

(38) *Tony.* It's a long, dark, boggy, dirty, dangerous way. Stingo, tell the gentlemen the way to Mr. Hardcastle's! (*Winking upon the* Landlord.) Mr. Hardcastle's, of Quagmire Marsh, you understand me.

(39) *Land.* Master Hardcastle's! Lock-a-daisy, my masters, you're come a deadly deal wrong! When you came to the bottom of the hill, you should have crossed down Squash Lane.

(40) *Mar.* Cross down Squash Lane!

(41) *Land.* Then you were to keep straight forward, till you came to four roads.

(42) *Mar.* Come to where four roads meet?

(43) *Tony.* Ay; but you must be sure to take only one of them.

(44) *Mar.* O, sir, you're facetious.

(45) *Tony.* Then keeping to the right, you are to go side-ways till you come upon Crackskull Common: then you must look sharp for the track of the wheel, and go forward till you come to Farmer Murrain's barn. Coming to the farmer's barn, you are to turn to the right, and then to the left, and then to the right about again, till you find out the old mill—

(46) *Mar.* Why, man! we could as soon find out the longitude!

(47) *Hast.* What's to be done, Marlow?

(48) *Mar.* This house promises but a poor reception; though perhaps the landlord can accommodate us.

(49) *Land.* Alack, master, we have but one spare bed in the whole house.

(50) *Tony.* And to my knowledge, that's taken up by three lodgers already. (*After a pause, in which the rest seem disconcerted.*) I have hit it. Don't you think, Stingo, our landlady could accommodate the gentlemen by the fire-side, with —three chairs and a bolster?

(51) *Hast.* I hate sleeping by the fire-side.

(52) *Mar.* And I detest your three chairs and a bolster.

(53) *Tony.* You do, do you? then, let me see—what if you go on a mile further, to the Buck's Head; the old Buck's Head on the hill, one of the best inns in the whole county?

(54) *Hast.* O ho! so we have escaped an adventure for this night, however.

(55) *Land.* (*Apart to* TONY.) Sure, you ben't sending them to your father's as an inn, be you?

(56) *Tony.* Mum, you fool you. Let *them* find that out. (*To them.*) You have only to keep on straight forward, till you come to a large old house by the roadside. You'll see a pair of large horns over the door. That's the sign. Drive up the yard, and call stoutly about you.

(57) *Hast.* Sir, we are obliged to you. The servants can't miss the way?

(58) *Tony.* No, no: but I tell you, though, the landlord is rich, and going to leave off business; so he wants to be thought a gentleman, saving your presence, he! he! he! He'll be for giving you his company; and, 'faith, if you mind him, he'll persuade you that his mother was an alderman, and his aunt a justice of peace.

(59) *Land.* A troublesome old blade, to be sure; but a keeps as good wines and beds as any in the whole country.

(60) *Mar.* Well, if he supplies us with these, we shall want no further connection. We are to turn to the right, did you say?

(61) *Tony.* No, no; straight forward. I'll just step myself, and show you a piece of the way. (*To the* Landlord.) Mum!

(62) *Land.* Ah! bless your heart, for a sweet, pleasant—mischievous rascal.   [*Exeunt.*

ACT THE SECOND.

Scene—*An old-fashioned House.*

Enter Hardcastle, *followed by three or four awkward* Servants.

(1) *Hard.* Well, I hope you are perfect in the table exercise I have been teaching you these three days. You all know your posts and your places, and can show that you have been used to good company, without ever stirring from home.

(2) *Omnes.* Ay, ay.

(3) *Hard.* When company comes you are not to pop out and stare, and then run in again, like frighted rabbits in a warren.

(4) *Omnes.* No, no.

(5) *Hard.* You, Diggory, whom I have taken from the barn, are to make a show at the side-table; and you, Roger, whom I have advanced from the plough, are to place yourself behind my chair. But you're not to stand so, with your hands in your pockets. Take your hands from your pockets, Roger; and from your head, you blockhead you. See how Diggory carries his hands. They're a little too stiff, indeed, but that's no great matter.

(6) *Dig.* Ay, mind how I hold them. I learned to hold my hands this way when I was upon drill for the militia. And so being upon drill—

(7) *Hard.* You must not be so talkative, Diggory. You must be all attention to the guests. You must hear us talk, and not think of talking; you must see us drink, and not think of drinking; you must see us eat, and not think of eating.

(8) *Dig.* By the laws, your worship, that's parfectly un-

possible. Whenever Diggory sees yeating going forward, he's always wishing for a mouthful himself.

(9) *Hard.* Blockhead! Is not a bellyful in the kitchen as good as a bellyful in the parlour? Stay your stomach with that reflection.

(10) *Dig.* I thank your worship, I'll make a shift to stay my stomach with a slice of cold beef in the pantry.

(11) *Hard.* Diggory, you are too talkative.—Then, if I happen to say a good thing, or tell a good story at table, you must not all burst out a-laughing, as if you made part of the company.

(12) *Dig.* Then your worship must not tell the story of Ould Grouse in the gun-room: I can't help laughing at that —he! he! he!—for the soul of me. We have laughed at that these twenty years—ha! ha! ha!

(13) *Hard.* Ha! ha! ha! The story is a good one. Well, honest Diggory, you may laugh at that—but still remember to be attentive. Suppose one of the company should call for a glass of wine, how will you behave? A glass of wine, sir, if you please (*to* DIGGORY).—Eh, why don't you move?

(14) *Dig.* Your worship, I never have courage till I see the eatables and drinkables brought upo' the table, and then I'm as bauld as a lion.

(15) *Hard.* What, will nobody move?

(16) *First Serv.* I'm not to leave this pleace.

(17) *Second Serv.* I'm sure it's no pleace of mine

(18) *Third Serv.* Nor mine, for sartin.

(19) *Dig.* And I'm sure it canna be mine.

(20) *Hard.* You numskulls! and so while, like your betters, you are quarrelling for places, the guests must be starved. O you dunces! I find I must begin all over again—But don't I hear a coach drive into the yard? To your posts, you block-heads. I'll go in the mean time and give my old friend's son a hearty reception at the gate.   [*Exit* Hardcastle.

(21) *Dig.* By the elevens, my pleace is gone quite out of my head.

(22) *Rog.* I know that my pleace is to be everywhere.

(23) *First Serv.* Where is mine?

(24) *Second Serv.* My pleace is to be nowhere at all; and so Is' go about my business.

> [*Exeunt* Servants, *running about as if frighted, different ways.*

Enter Servant *with candles, showing in* MARLOW *and* HASTINGS.

(25) *Serv.* Welcome, gentlemen, very welcome! This way.

(26) *Hast.* After the disappointments of the day, welcome once more, Charles, to the comforts of a clean room and a good fire. Upon my word, a very well-looking house; antique but creditable.

(27) *Mar.* The usual fate of a large mansion. Having first ruined the master by good housekeeping, it at last comes to levy contributions as an inn.

(28) *Hast.* As you say, we passengers are to be taxed to pay all these fineries. I have often seen a good sideboard, or a marble chimney-piece, though not actually put in the bill, inflame a reckoning confoundedly.

(29) *Mar.* Travellers, George, must pay in all places: the only difference is, that in good inns you pay dearly for luxuries; in bad inns you are fleeced and starved.

(30) *Hast.* You have lived very much among them. In truth, I have been often surprised, that you who have seen so much of the world, with your natural good sense, and your many opportunities, could never yet acquire a requisite share of assurance.

(31) *Mar.* The Englishman's malady. But tell me, George, where could I have learned that assurance you talk of? My life has been chiefly spent in a college or an inn, in seclusion from that lovely part of the creation that chiefly teach men confidence. I don't know that I was ever familiarly acquainted with a single modest woman—except my mother—But among females of another class, you know—

(32) *Hast.* Ay, among them you are impudent enough of all conscience.

(33) *Mar.* They are of *us*, you know.

(34) *Hast.* But in the company of women of reputation I

never saw such an idiot, such a trembler; you look for all the world as if you wanted an opportunity of stealing out of the room.

(35) *Mar.* Why, man, that's because I do want to steal out of the room. Faith, I have often formed a resolution to break the ice, and rattle away at any rate. But I don't know how, a single glance from a pair of fine eyes has totally overset my resolution. An impudent fellow may counterfeit modesty; but I'll be hanged if a modest man can ever counterfeit impudence.

(36) *Hast.* If you could but say half the fine things to them that I have heard you lavish upon the bar-maid of an inn, or even a college bed-maker—

(37) *Mar.* Why, George, I can't say fine things to them; they freeze, they petrify me. They may talk of a comet, or a burning mountain, or some such bagatelle; but, to me, a modest woman, drest out in all her finery, is the most tremendous object of the whole creation.

(38) *Hast.* Ha! ha! ha! At this rate, man, how can you ever expect to marry?

(39) *Mar.* Never; unless, as among kings and princes, my bride were to be courted by proxy. If, indeed, like an Eastern bridegroom, one were to be introduced to a wife he never saw before, it might be endured. But to go through all the terrors of a formal courtship, together with the episode of aunts, grandmothers, and cousins, and at last to blurt out the broad staring question of, Madam, will you marry me? No, no, that's a strain much above me, I assure you.

(40) *Hast.* I pity you. But how do you intend behaving to the lady you are come down to visit at the request of your father.

(41) *Mar.* As I behave to all other ladies. Bow very low, answer yes or no to all her demands—But for the rest—I don't think I shall venture to look in her face till I see my father's again.

(42) *Hast.* I'm surprised that one who is so warm a friend can be so cool a lover.

(43) *Mar.* To be explicit, my dear Hastings, my chief

inducement down was to be instrumental in forwarding your happiness, not my own. Miss Neville loves you, the family don't know you; as my friend you are sure of a reception, and let honour do the rest.

(44) *Hast.* My dear Marlow! But I'll suppress the emotion. Were I a wretch, meanly seeking to carry off a fortune, you should be the last man in the world I would apply to for assistance. But Miss Neville's person is all I ask, and that is mine, both from her deceased father's consent, and her own inclination.

(45) *Mar.* Happy man! You have talents and art to captivate any woman. I'm doomed to adore the sex, and yet to converse with the only part of it I despise. This stammer in my address, and this awkward prepossessing visage of mine, can never permit me to soar above the reach of a milliner's 'prentice, or one of the duchesses of Drury-lane. Pshaw! this fellow here to interrupt us.

Enter HARDCASTLE.

(46) *Hard.* Gentlemen, once more you are heartily welcome. Which is Mr. Marlow? Sir, you are heartily welcome. It's not my way, you see, to receive my friends with my back to the fire. I like to give them a hearty reception in the old style at my gate. I like to see their horses and trunks taken care of.

(47) *Mar.* (*Aside.*) He has got our names from the servants already. (*To him.*) We approve your caution and hospitality, sir. (*To Hastings.*) I have been thinking, George, of changing our travelling dresses in the morning. I am grown confoundedly ashamed of mine.

(48) *Hard.* I beg, Mr. Marlow, you'll use no ceremony in this house.

(49) *Hast.* I fancy, Charles, you're right; the first blow is half the battle. I intend opening the campaign with the white and gold.

(50) *Hard.* Mr. Marlow—Mr. Hastings—gentlemen—pray be under no restraint in this house. This is Liberty-hall, gentlemen. You may do just as you please here.

(51) *Mar.* Yet, George, if we open the campaign too fiercely at first, we may want ammunition before it is over. I think to reserve the embroidery to secure a retreat.

(52) *Hard.* Your talking of a retreat, Mr. Marlow, puts me in mind of the Duke of Marlborough, when he went to besiege Denain. He first summoned the garrison—

(53) *Mar.* Don't you think the *ventre d'or* waistcoat will do with the plain brown?

(54) *Hard.* He first summoned the garrison, which might consist of about five thousand men—

(55) *Hast.* I think not: brown and yellow mix but very poorly.

(56) *Hard.* I say, gentlemen, as I was telling you, he summoned the garrison, which might consist of about five thousand men—

(57) *Mar.* The girls like finery.

(58) *Hard.* Which might consist of about five thousand men, well appointed with stores, ammunition, and other implements of war. Now, says the Duke of Marlborough to George Brooks, that stood next to him—you must have heard of George Brooks—I'll pawn my dukedom, says he, but I take that garrison without spilling a drop of blood. So—

(59) *Mar.* What, my good friend, if you give us a glass of punch in the meantime; it would help us to carry on the siege with vigour.

(60) *Hard.* Punch, sir! (*Aside.*) This is the most unaccountable kind of modesty I ever met with.

(61) *Mar.* Yes, sir, punch. A glass of warm punch, after our journey, will be comfortable. This is Liberty-hall, you know.

(62) *Hard.* Here's a cup, sir.

(63) *Mar.* (*Aside.*) So this fellow, in his Liberty-hall, will only let us have just what he pleases.

(64) *Hard.* (*Taking the cup.*) I hope you'll find it to your mind. I have prepared it with my own hands, and I believe you'll own the ingredients are tolerable. Will you be so good as to pledge me, sir? Here, Mr. Marlow, here is to our better acquaintance.   [*Drinks.*

(65) *Mar.* (*Aside.*) A very impudent fellow this! but he's a character, and I'll humour him a little. Sir, my service to you.   [*Drinks.*

(66) *Hast.* (*Aside.*) I see this fellow wants to give us his company, and forgets that he's an innkeeper, before he has learned to be a gentleman.

(67) *Mar.* From the excellence of your cup, my old friend, I suppose you have a good deal of business in this part of the country. Warm work, now and then, at elections, I suppose.

(68) *Hard.* No, sir, I have long given that work over. Since our betters have hit upon the expedient of electing each other, there is no business " for us that sell ale."

(69) *Hast.* So, then, you have no turn for politics, I find.

(70) *Hard.* Not in the least. There was a time, indeed, I fretted myself about the mistakes of government, like other people; but finding myself every day grow more angry, and the government growing no better, I left it to mend itself. Since that, I no more trouble my head about Hyder Ally, or Ally Cawn, than about Ally Croaker. Sir, my service to you.

(71) *Hast.* So that with eating above stairs, and drinking below, with receiving your friends within, and amusing them without, you lead a good pleasant bustling life of it.

(72) *Hard.* I do stir about a great deal, that's certain. Half the differences of the parish are adjusted in this very parlour.

(73) *Mar.* (*After drinking.*) And you have an argument in your cup, old gentleman, better than any in Westminster-hall.

(74) *Hard.* Ay, young gentleman, that, and a little philosophy.

(75) *Mar.* (*Aside.*) Well, this is the first time I ever heard of an innkeeper's philosophy.

(76) *Hast.* So then, like an experienced general, you attack them on every quarter. If you find their reason manageable, you attack it with your philosophy; if you find they have no reason, you attack them with this. Here's your health, my philosopher.   [*Drinks.*

(77) *Hard.* Good, very good, thank you; ha! ha! Your

generalship puts me in mind of Prince Eugene, when he fought the Turks at the battle of Belgrade. You shall hear.

(78) *Mar.* Instead of the battle of Belgrade, I believe it's almost time to talk about supper. What has your philosophy got in the house for supper?

(79) *Hard.* For supper, sir? (*Aside.*) Was ever such a request to a man in his own house?

(80) *Mar.* Yes, sir, supper, sir; I begin to feel an appetite. I shall make fine work to-night in the larder, I promise you.

(81) *Hard.* (*Aside.*) Such a brazen dog sure never my eyes beheld. [*To him.*] Why, really, sir, as for supper I can't well tell. My Dorothy and the cook-maid settle these things between them. I leave these kind of things entirely to them.

(82) *Mar.* You do, do you?

(83) *Hard.* Entirely. By the bye, I believe they are in actual consultation upon what's for supper this moment in the kitchen.

(84) *Mar.* Then I beg they'll admit me as one of their privy council. It's a way I have got. When I travel, I always choose to regulate my own supper. Let the cook be called. No offence, I hope, sir.

(85) *Hard.* O no, sir, none in the least; yet I don't know how; our Bridget, the cook-maid, is not very communicative upon these occasions. Should we send for her, she might scold us all out of the house.

(86) *Hast.* Let's see your list of the larder then. I ask it as a favour. I always match my appetite to my bill of fare.

(87) *Mar.* [*To* HARDCASTLE, *who looks at them with surprise.*] Sir, he's very right, and it's my way too.

(88) *Hard.* Sir, you have a right to command here. Here, Roger, bring us the bill of fare for to-night's supper: I believe it's drawn out—Your manner, Mr. Hastings, puts me in mind of my uncle, Colonel Wallop. It was a saying of his, that no man was sure of his supper till he had eaten it.

(89) *Hast.* (*Aside.*) All upon the high rope! His uncle a colonel! we shall soon hear of his mother being a justice of the peace. But let's hear the bill of fare.

(90) *Mar.* (*Perusing.*) What's here? For the first course;

for the second course; for the dessert. The mischief, sir; do you think we have brought down a whole Joiners' Company, or the corporation of Bedford, to eat up such a supper? Two or three little things, clean and comfortable, will do.

(91) *Hast.* But let's hear it.

(92) *Mar.* (*Reading.*) For the first course, at the top, a pig and prune sauce.

(93) *Hast.* Hang your pig, I say.

(94) *Mar.* And hang your prune sauce, say I.

(95) *Hard.* And yet, gentlemen, to men that are hungry, pig with prune sauce is very good eating.

(96) *Mar.* At the bottom, a calf's tongue and brains.

(97) *Hast.* Let your brains be knocked out, my good sir, I don't like them.

(98) *Mar.* Or you may clap them on a plate by themselves. I do.

(99) *Hard.* (*Aside.*) Their impudence confounds me. [*To them.*] Gentlemen, you are my guests, make what alterations you please. Is there anything else you wish to retrench or alter, gentlemen?

(100) *Mar.* Item, a pork pie, a boiled rabbit and sausages, a Florentine, a shaking pudding, and a dish of tiff—taff—taffety cream.

(101) *Hast.* Confound your made dishes; I shall be as much at a loss in this house as at a green and yellow dinner at the French ambassador's table. I'm for plain eating.

(102) *Hard.* I'm sorry, gentlemen, that I have nothing you like, but if there be anything you have a particular fancy to—

(103) *Mar.* Why, really sir, your bill of fare is so exquisite, that any one part of it is full as good as another. Send us what you please. So much for supper. And now to see that our beds are aired, and properly taken care of.

(104) *Hard.* I entreat you'll leave that to me. You shall not stir a step.

(105) *Mar.* Leave that to you! I protest, sir, you must excuse me, I always look to these things myself.

(106) *Hard.* I must insist, sir, you'll make yourself easy on that head.

(107) *Mar.* You see I'm resolved on it. (*Aside.*) A very troublesome fellow this, as I ever met with.

(108) *Hard.* Well, sir, I'm resolved at least to attend you. (*Aside.*) This may be modern modesty, but I never saw anything look so like old-fashioned impudence.

[*Exeunt* Marlow *and* Hardcastle.

(109) *Hast.* (*Alone.*) So, I find this fellow's civilities begin to grow troublesome. But who can be angry at those assiduities which are meant to please him? Ha! what do I see? Miss Neville, by all that's happy!

Enter MISS NEVILLE.

(110) *Miss Nev.* My dear Hastings! To what unexpected good fortune, to what accident, am I to ascribe this happy meeting?

(111) *Hast.* Rather let me ask the same question, as I could never have hoped to meet my dearest Constance at an inn.

(112) *Miss Nev.* An inn! sure you mistake: my aunt, my guardian, lives here. What could induce you to think this house an inn?

(113) *Hast.* My friend, Mr. Marlow, with whom I came down, and I, have been sent here as to an inn, I assure you. A young fellow, whom we accidentally met at a house hard by, directed us hither.

(114) *Miss Nev.* Certainly it must be one of my hopeful cousin's tricks, of whom you have heard me talk so often; ha! ha! ha!

(115) *Hast.* He whom your aunt intends for you? he of whom I have such just apprehensions?

(116) *Miss Nev.* You have nothing to fear from him, I assure you. You'd adore him, if you knew how heartily he despises me. My aunt knows it too, and has undertaken to court me for him, and actually begins to think she has made a conquest.

(117) *Hast.* Thou dear dissembler! You must know, my Constance, I have just seized this happy opportunity of my friend's visit here to get admittance into the family. The horses that carried us down are now fatigued with their journey, but they'll soon be refreshed; and then, if my dearest

girl will trust in her faithful Hastings, we shall soon be landed in France, where even among slaves the laws of marriage are respected.

(118) *Miss Nev.* I have often told you, that though ready to obey you, I yet should leave my little fortune behind with reluctance. The greatest part of it was left me by my uncle, the India director, and chiefly consists in jewels. I have been for some time persuading my aunt to let me wear them. I fancy I'm very near succeeding. The instant they are put into my possession, you shall find me ready to make them and myself yours.

(119) *Hast.* Perish the baubles! Your person is all I desire. In the meantime, my friend Marlow must not be let into his mistake. I know the strange reserve of his temper is such, that if abruptly informed of it, he would instantly quit the house before our plan was ripe for execution.

(120) *Miss Nev.* But how shall we keep him in the deception? Miss Hardcastle is just returned from walking; what if we still continue to deceive him?—This, this way—

[*They confer.*

Enter MARLOW.

(121) *Mar.* The assiduities of these good people teaze me beyond bearing. My host seems to think it ill manners to leave me alone, and so he claps not only himself, but his old-fashioned wife, on my back. They talk of coming to sup with us too; and then, I suppose, we are to run the gauntlet through all the rest of the family.—What have we got here?

(122) *Hast.* My dear Charles! Let me congratulate you!— The most fortunate accident!— Who do you think is just alighted?

(123) *Mar.* Cannot guess.

(124) *Hast.* Our mistresses, boy, Miss Hardcastle and Miss Neville. Give me leave to introduce Miss Constance Neville to your acquaintance. Happening to dine in the neighbourhood, they called on their return to take fresh horses here. Miss Hardcastle has just stept into the next room, and will be back in an instant. Wasn't it lucky? eh!

(125) *Mar.* (*Aside.*) I have been mortified enough of all conscience, and here comes something to complete my embarrassment.

(126) *Hast.* Well, but wasn't it the most fortunate thing in the world?

(127) *Mar.* Oh! yes. Very fortunate—a most joyful encounter—But our dresses, George, you know, are in disorder—What if we should postpone the happiness till to-morrow?—To-morrow at her own house—It will be every bit as convenient—and rather more respectful—To-morrow let it be.

[*Offering to go.*

(128) *Miss Nev.* By no means, sir. Your ceremony will displease her. The disorder of your dress will show the ardour of your impatience. Besides, she knows you are in the house, and will permit you to see her.

(129) *Mar.* O! how shall I support it? Hem! hem! Hastings, you must not go. You are to assist me, you know. I shall be confoundedly ridiculous. Yet, hang it! I'll take courage. Hem!

(130) *Hast.* Pshaw, man! it's but the first plunge, and all's over. She's but a woman, you know.

(131) *Mar.* And, of all women, she that I dread most to encounter.

Enter MISS HARDCASTLE, *as returned from walking,*
a bonnet, &c.

(132) *Hast.* (*Introducing them.*) Miss Hardcastle, Mr. Marlow. I'm proud of bringing two persons of such merit together, that only want to know, to esteem each other.

(133) *Miss Hard.* (*Aside.*) Now for meeting my modest gentleman with a demure face, and quite in his own manner. (*After a pause, in which he appears very uneasy and disconcerted.*) I'm glad of your safe arrival, sir. I'm told you had some accidents by the way.

(134) *Mar.* Only a few, madam. Yes, we had some. Yes, madam, a good many accidents, but should be sorry—madam—or rather glad of any accidents—that are so agreeably concluded. Hem!

(135) *Hast.* (*To him.*) You never spoke better in your whole life. Keep it up, and I'll insure you the victory.

(136) *Miss Hard.* I'm afraid you flatter, sir. You that have seen so much of the finest company, can find little entertainment in an obscure corner of the country.

(137) *Mar.* (*Gathering courage.*) I have lived, indeed, in the world, madam; but I have kept very little company. I have been but an observer upon life, madam, while others were enjoying it.

(138) *Miss Nev.* But that, I am told, is the way to enjoy it at last.

(139) *Hast.* (*To him.*) Cicero never spoke better. Once more, and you are confirmed in assurance for ever.

(140) *Mar.* (*To him.*) Hem! Stand by me, then, and when I'm down, throw in a word or two, to set me up again.

(141) *Miss Hard.* An observer, like you, upon life were, I fear, disagreeably employed, since you must have had much more to censure than to approve.

(142) *Mar.* Pardon me, madam. I was always willing to be amused. The folly of most people is rather an object of mirth than uneasiness.

(143) *Hast.* (*To him.*) Bravo, bravo. Never spoke so well in your whole life. Well, Miss Hardcastle, I see that you and Mr. Marlow are going to be very good company. I believe our being here will but embarrass the interview.

(144) *Mar.* Not in the least, Mr. Hastings. We like your company of all things. (*To him.*) What! George, sure you won't go? how can you leave us?

(145) *Hast.* Our presence will but spoil conversation, so we'll retire to the next room. (*To him.*) You don't consider, man, that we are to manage a little *tête-à-tête* of our own. [*Exeunt.*

(146) *Miss Hard.* (*after a pause*). But you have not been wholly an observer, I presume, sir; the ladies, I should hope, have employed some part of your addresses.

(147) *Mar.* (*Relapsing into timidity.*) Pardon me, madam, I—I—I—as yet have studied—only—to—deserve them.

(148) *Miss Hard.* And that, some say, is the very worst way to obtain them.

(149) *Mar.* Perhaps so, madam. But I love to converse only with the more grave and sensible part of the sex. But I'm afraid I grow tiresome.

(150) *Miss Hard.* Not at all, sir; there is nothing I like so much as grave conversation myself; I could hear it for ever. Indeed, I have often been surprised how a man of sentiment could ever admire those light airy pleasures, where nothing reaches the heart.

(151) *Mar.* It's—a disease—of the mind, madam. In the variety of tastes there must be some who, wanting a relish—for—um—a—um.

(152) *Miss Hard.* I understand you, sir. There must be some who, wanting a relish for refined pleasures, pretend to despise what they are incapable of tasting.

(153) *Mar.* My meaning, madam, but infinitely better expressed. And I can't help observing—a—

(154) *Miss Hard.* (*Aside.*) Who could ever suppose this fellow impudent upon some occasions? (*To him.*) You were going to observe, sir—

(155) *Mar.* I was observing, madam—I protest, madam, I forget what I was going to observe.

(156) *Miss Hard.* (*Aside.*) I vow and so do I. (*To him.*) You were observing, sir, that in this age of hypocrisy—something about hypocrisy, sir.

(157) *Mar.* Yes, madam, in this age of hypocrisy there are few who upon strict inquiry do not—a—a—a

(158) *Miss Hard.* I understand you perfectly, sir.

(159) *Mar.* (*Aside.*) Faith! and that's more than I do myself.

(160) *Miss Hard.* You mean that in this hypocritical age there are few that do not condemn in public what they practise in private, and think they pay every debt to virtue when they praise it.

(161) *Mar.* True, madam; those who have most virtue in their mouths, have least of it in their bosoms. But I'm sure I tire you, madam.

(162) *Miss Hard.* Not in the least, sir; there's something so agreeable and spirited in your manner, such life and force—pray, sir, go on.

(163) *Mar.* Yes, madam. I was saying—that there are some occasions, when a total want of courage, madam, destroys all the—and puts us—upon a—a—a—

(164) *Miss Hard.* I agree with you entirely; a want of courage upon some occasions assumes the appearance of ignorance, and betrays us when we most want to excel. I beg you'll proceed.

(165) *Mar.* Yes, madam. Morally speaking, madam—But I see Miss Neville expecting us in the next room. I would not intrude for the world.

(166) *Miss Hard.* I protest, sir, I never was more agreeably entertained in all my life. Pray go on.

(167) *Mar.* Yes, madam, I was—But she beckons us to join her. Madam, shall I do myself the honour to attend you!

(168) *Miss Hard.* Well, then, I'll follow.

(169) *Mar.* (*Aside.*) This pretty smooth dialogue has done for me.   [*Exit.*

(170) *Miss Hard.* (*Alone.*) Ha! ha! ha! Was there ever such a sober, sentimental interview? I'm certain he scarce looked in my face the whole time. Yet the fellow, but for his unaccountable bashfulness, is pretty well too. He has good sense, but then so buried in his fears, that it fatigues one more than ignorance. If I could teach him a little confidence, it would be doing somebody that I know of a piece of service. But who is that somebody?—That, faith, is a question I can scarce answer.   [*Exit.*

Enter TONY *and* MISS NEVILLE, *followed by* MRS.
HARDCASTLE *and* HASTINGS.

(171) *Tony.* What do you follow me for, cousin Con? I wonder you're not ashamed to be so very engaging.

(172) *Miss Nev.* I hope, cousin, one may speak to one's own relations and not be to blame.

(173) *Tony.* Ay, but I know what sort of a relation you want to make me, though; but it won't do. I tell you, cousin Con, it won't do; so I beg you'll keep your distance, I want no nearer relationship.

[*She follows, coquetting him to the back scene.*

(174) *Mrs. Hard.* Well! I vow, Mr. Hastings, you are very entertaining. There's nothing in the world I love to talk of so much as London, and the fashions, though I was never there myself.

(175) *Hast.* Never there! You amaze me. From your air and manner, I concluded you had been bred all your life either at Ranelagh, St. James's, or Tower Wharf.

(176) *Mrs. Hard.* O! sir, you're only pleased to say so. We country persons can have no manner at all. I'm in love with the town, and that serves to raise me above some of our neighbouring rustics; but who can have a manner, that has never seen the Pantheon, the Grotto Gardens, the Borough, and such places where the nobility chiefly resort? All I can do is to enjoy London at second-hand. I take care to know every *tête-à-tête* from the Scandalous Magazine, and have all the fashions, as they come out, in a letter from the two Miss Rickets of Crooked Lane. Pray how do you like this head, Mr. Hastings?

(177) *Hast.* Extremely elegant and *dégagée*, upon my word, madam. Your friseur is a Frenchman, I suppose?

(178) *Mrs. Hard.* I protest, I dressed it myself from a print in the Ladies' Memorandum-book for the last year.

(179) *Hast.* Indeed! Such a head in a side-box at the playhouse would draw as many gazers as my Lady Mayoress at a City Ball.

(180) *Mrs. Hard.* I vow, since inoculation began, there is no such thing to be seen as a plain woman; so one must dress a little particular, or one may escape in the crowd.

(181) *Hast.* But that can never be your case, madam, in any dress. (*Bowing.*)

(182) *Mrs. Hard.* Yet, what signifies my dressing when I have such a piece of antiquity by my side as Mr. Hardcastle: all I can say will never argue down a single button from his clothes. I have often wanted him to throw off his great flaxen wig, and where he was bald, to plaster it over, like my Lord Pately, with powder.

(183) *Hast.* You are right, madam; for, as among the ladies there are none ugly, so among the men there are none old.

(253)   B

(184) *Mrs. Hard.* But what do you think his answer was? Why, with his usual Gothic vivacity, he said I only wanted him to throw off his wig, to convert it into a *tête* for my own wearing.

(185) *Hast.* Intolerable! At your age you may wear what you please, and it must become you.

(186) *Mrs. Hard.* Pray, Mr. Hastings, what do you take to be the most fashionable age about town?

(187) *Hast.* Some time ago, forty was all the mode; but I'm told the ladies intend to bring up fifty for the ensuing winter.

(188) *Mrs. Hard.* Seriously. Then I shall be too young for the fashion.

(189) *Hast.* No lady begins now to put on jewels till she's past forty. For instance, Miss there, in a polite circle, would be considered as a child, as a mere maker of samplers.

(190) *Mrs. Hard.* And yet Mrs. Niece thinks herself as much a woman, and is as fond of jewels, as the oldest of us all.

(191) *Hast.* Your niece, is she? And that young gentleman, a brother of yours, I should presume?

(192) *Mrs. Hard.* My son, sir. They are contracted to each other. Observe their little sports. They fall in and out ten times a day, as if they were man and wife already. (*To them.*) Well, Tony, child, what soft things are you saying to your cousin Constance this evening?

(193) *Tony.* I have been saying no soft things; but that it's very hard to be followed about so. I've not a place in the house now that's left to myself, but the stable.

(194) *Mrs. Hard.* Never mind him, Con, my dear. He's in another story behind your back.

(195) *Miss Nev.* There's something generous in my cousin's manner. He falls out before faces to be forgiven in private.

(196) *Tony.* That's a confounded—crack.

(197) *Mrs. Hard.* Ah! he's a sly one. Don't you think they are like each other about the mouth, Mr. Hastings? The Blenkinsop mouth to a T. They're of a size too. Back to back, my pretties, that Mr. Hastings may see you. Come, Tony.

(198) *Tony.* You had as good not make me, I tell you. (*Measuring.*)

(199) *Miss Nev.* O dear! he has almost cracked my head.

(200) *Mrs. Hard.* O, the monster! For shame, Tony. You a man, and behave so!

(201) *Tony.* If I'm a man, let me have my fortin. I'll not be made a fool of no longer.

(202) *Mrs. Hard.* Is this, ungrateful boy, all that I'm to get for the pains I have taken in your education? I that have rocked you in your cradle, and fed that pretty mouth with a spoon! Did not I work that waistcoat to make you genteel? Did not I prescribe for you every day, and weep while the receipt was operating?

(203) *Tony.* You had reason to weep, for you have been dosing me ever since I was born. I have gone through every receipt in the Complete Huswife ten times over; and you have thoughts of coursing me through Quincy next spring. But, I tell you, I'll not be made a fool of no longer.

(204) *Mrs. Hard.* Wasn't it all for your good, viper? Wasn't it all for your good?

(205) *Tony.* I wish you'd let me and my good alone, then. Snubbing this way when I'm in spirits. If I'm to have any good, let it come of itself; not to keep dinging it, dinging it into one so.

(206) *Mrs. Hard.* That's false; I never see you when you're in spirits. No, Tony, you then go to the alehouse or kennel. I'm never to be delighted with you're agreeable wild notes, unfeeling monster!

(207) *Tony.* Mamma, your own notes are the wildest of the two.

(208) *Mrs. Hard.* Was ever the like? But I see he wants to break my heart, I see he does.

(209) *Hast.* Dear madam, permit me to lecture the young gentleman a little. I'm certain I can persuade him to his duty.

(210) *Mrs. Hard.* Well, I must retire. Come, Constance, my love. You see, Mr. Hastings, the wretchedness of my situation: was ever poor woman so plagued with a dear, sweet, pretty, provoking, undutiful boy?

[*Exeunt* Mrs. Hardcastle *and* Miss Neville.

(211) *Tony.* (*Singing.*) " There was a young man riding by,

and fain would have his will. Rang do didlo dee."—Don't mind her. Let her cry. It's the comfort of her heart. I have seen her and sister cry over a book for an hour together; and they said they liked the book the better the more it made them cry.

(212) *Hast.* Then you're no friend to the ladies, I find, my pretty young gentleman.

(213) *Tony.* That's as I find 'um.

(214) *Hast.* Not to her of your mother's choosing, I dare answer? And yet she appears to me a pretty well-tempered girl.

(215) *Tony.* That's because you don't know her as well as I. I know every inch about her; and there's not a more bitter cantackerous toad in all Christendom.

(216) *Hast.* (*Aside.*) Pretty encouragement this for a lover!

(217) *Tony.* I have seen her since the height of that. She has as many tricks as a hare in a thicket, or a colt the first day's breaking.

(218) *Hast.* To me she appears sensible and silent.

(219) *Tony.* Ay, before company. But when she's with her playmate, she's as loud as a hog in a gate.

(220) *Hast.* But there is a meek modesty about her that charms me.

(221) *Tony.* Yes, but curb her never so little, she kicks up, and you're flung in a ditch.

(222) *Hast.* Well, but you must allow her a little beauty.— Yes, you must allow her some beauty.

(223) *Tony.* Bandbox! She's all a made-up thing, mun. Ah! could you but see Bet Bouncer of these parts, you might then talk of beauty. Faith, she has two eyes as black as sloes, and cheeks as broad and red as a pulpit cushion. She'd make two of she.

(224) *Hast.* Well, what say you to a friend that would take this bitter bargain off your hands?

(225) *Tony.* Anon.

(226) *Hast.* Would you thank him that would take Miss Neville, and leave you to happiness and your dear Betsy?

(227) *Tony.* Ay; but where is there such a friend, for who would take her?

(228) *Hast.* I am he. If you but assist me, I'll engage to whip her off to France, and you shall never hear more of her.

(229) *Tony.* Assist you! I will, to the last drop of my blood. I'll clap a pair of horses to your chaise that shall trundle you off in a twinkling, and may be get you a part of her fortin beside, in jewels, that you little dream of.

(230) *Hast.* My dear 'squire, this looks like a lad of spirit.

(231) *Tony.* Come along, then, and you shall see more of my spirit before you have done with me. (*Singing.*)

> "We are the boys
> That fear no noise
> Where the thundering cannons roar."

[*Exeunt.*

ACT THE THIRD.

Scene.—*The same.*

Enter HARDCASTLE, alone.

(1) *Hard.* What could my old friend Sir Charles mean by recommending his son as the modestest young man in town? To me he appears the most impudent piece of brass that ever spoke with a tongue. He has taken possession of the easy-chair by the fireside already. He took off his boots in the parlour, and desired me to see them taken care of. I'm desirous to know how his impudence affects my daughter. She will certainly be shocked at it.

Enter MISS HARDCASTLE, *plainly dressed.*

(2) *Hard.* Well, my Kate, I see you have changed your dress, as I bade you; and yet, I believe, there was no great occasion.

(3) *Miss Hard.* I find such a pleasure, sir, in obeying your commands, that I take care to observe them without ever debating their propriety.

(4) *Hard.* And yet, Kate, I sometimes give you some cause, particularly when I recommended my modest gentleman to you as a lover to-day.

(5) *Miss Hard.* You taught me to expect something extraordinary, and I find the original exceeds the description.

(6) *Hard.* I was never so surprised in my life! He has quite confounded all my faculties!

(7) *Miss Hard.* I never saw anything like it: and a man of the world too!

(8) *Hard.* Ay, he learned it all abroad—what a fool was I, to think a young man could learn modesty by travelling. He might as soon learn wit at a masquerade.

(9) *Miss Hard.* It seems all natural to him.

(10) *Hard.* A good deal assisted by bad company and a French dancing-master.

(11) *Miss Hard.* Sure you mistake, papa! A French dancing-master could never have taught him that timid look —that awkward address—that bashful manner—

(12) *Hard.* Whose look? whose manner, child?

(13) *Miss Hard.* Mr. Marlow's: his *mauvaise honte*, his timidity, struck me at the first sight.

(14) *Hard.* Then your first sight deceived you; for I think him one of the most brazen first sights that ever astonished my senses.

(15) *Miss Hard.* Sure, sir, you rally! I never saw any one so modest.

(16) *Hard.* And can you be serious? I never saw such a bouncing, swaggering puppy since I was born. Bully Dawson was but a fool to him.

(17) *Miss Hard.* Surprising! He met me with a respectful bow, a stammering voice, and a look fixed on the ground.

(18) *Hard.* He met me with a loud voice, a lordly air, and a familiarity that made my blood freeze again.

(19) *Miss Hard.* He treated me with diffidence and respect; censured the manners of the age; admired the prudence of girls that never laughed; tired me with apologies for being tiresome; then left the room with a bow, and "Madam, I would not for the world detain you."

(20) *Hard.* He spoke to me as if he knew me all his life before; asked twenty questions, and never waited for an answer; interrupted my best remarks with some silly pun;

and when I was in my best story of the Duke of Marlborough and Prince Eugene, he asked if I had not a good hand at making punch. Yes, Kate, he asked your father if he was a maker of punch!

(21) *Miss Hard.* One of us must certainly be mistaken.

(22) *Hard.* If he be what he has shown himself, I'm determined he shall never have my consent.

(23) *Miss Hard.* And if he be the sullen thing I take him, he shall never have mine.

(24) *Hard.* In one thing then we are agreed—to reject him.

(25) *Miss Hard.* Yes; but upon conditions. For if you should find him less impudent, and I more presuming—if you find him more respectful, and I more importunate—I don't know—the fellow is well enough for a man—Certainly, we don't meet many such at a horse-race in the country.

(26) *Hard.* If we should find him so—But that's impossible. The first appearance has done my business. I'm seldom deceived in that.

(27) *Miss Hard.* And yet there may be many good qualities under that first appearance.

(28) *Hard.* Ay, when a girl finds a fellow's outside to her taste, she then sets about guessing the rest of his furniture. With her, a smooth face stands for good sense, and a genteel figure for every virtue.

(29) *Miss Hard.* I hope, sir, a conversation begun with a compliment to my good sense, won't end with a sneer at my understanding?

(30) *Hard.* Pardon me, Kate. But if young Mr. Brazen can find the art of reconciling contradictions, he may please us both, perhaps.

(31) *Miss Hard.* And as one of us must be mistaken, what if we go to make further discoveries?

(32) *Hard.* Agreed. But depend on't I'm in the right.

(33) *Miss Hard.* And depend on't I'm not much in the wrong. 　　　　　　　　　　　　　　　　　　　　*[Exeunt.*

Enter TONY *running in with a casket.*

(34) *Tony.* Well, I have got them. Here they are. My cousin Con's necklaces, bobs and all. My mother sha'n't cheat

the poor souls out of their fortin neither. O! my genus, is that you?

Enter HASTINGS.

(35) *Hast.* My dear friend, how have you managed with you mother? I hope you have amused her with pretending love for your cousin, and that you are willing to be reconciled at last? Our horses will be refreshed in a short time, and we shall soon be ready to set off.

(36) *Tony.* And here's something to bear your charges by the way (*giving the casket*); your sweetheart's jewels. Keep them; and hang those, I say, that would rob you of one of them.

(37) *Hast.* But how have you procured them from your mother?

(38) *Tony.* Ask me no questions, and I'll tell you no fibs. I procured them by the rule of thumb. If I had not a key to every drawer in mother's bureau, how could I go to the alehouse so often as I do? An honest man may rob himself of his own at any time.

(39) *Hast.* Thousands do it every day. But to be plain with you; Miss Neville is endeavouring to procure them from her aunt this very instant. If she succeeds, it will be the most delicate way at least of obtaining them.

(40) *Tony.* Well, keep them till you know how it will be. But I know how it will be well enough; she'd as soon part with the only sound tooth in her head.

(41) *Hast.* But I dread the effects of her resentment, when she finds she has lost them.

(42) *Tony.* Never you mind her resentment, leave *me* to manage that. I don't value her resentment the bounce of a cracker. Why, here they are. Morrice! Prance!

[*Exit* HASTINGS.

Enter MRS. HARDCASTLE *and* MISS NEVILLE.

(43) *Mrs. Hard.* Indeed, Constance, you amaze me. Such a girl as you want jewels! It will be time enough for jewels, my dear, twenty years hence, when your beauty begins to want repairs.

(44) *Miss Nev.* But what will repair beauty at forty, will certainly improve it at twenty, madam.

(45) *Mrs. Hard.* Yours, my dear, can admit of none. That natural blush is beyond a thousand ornaments. Besides, child, jewels are quite out at present. Don't you see half the ladies of our acquaintance, my Lady Kill-daylight, and Mrs. Crumb, and the rest of them, carry their jewels to town, and bring nothing but paste and marcasites back.

(46) *Miss Nev.* But who knows, madam, but somebody that shall be nameless would like me best with all my little finery about me?

(47) *Mrs. Hard.* Consult your glass, my dear, and then see if, with such a pair of eyes, you want any better sparklers. What do you think, Tony, my dear? Does your cousin Con want any jewels in your eyes to set off her beauty?

(48) *Tony.* That's as thereafter may be.

(49) *Miss Nev.* My dear aunt, if you knew how it would oblige me.

(50) *Mrs. Hard.* A parcel of old fashioned rose and table-cut things. They would make you look like the court of King Solomon at a puppet-show. Besides, I believe I can't readily come at them. They may be missing, for aught I know to the contrary.

(51) *Tony.* (*Apart to* MRS. HARDCASTLE.) Then why don't you tell her so at once, as she's so longing for them? Tell her they're lost. It's the only way to quiet her. Say they're lost, and call me to bear witness.

(52) *Mrs. Hard.* (*Apart to* TONY.) You know, my dear, I'm only keeping them for you. So if I say they're gone, you'll bear me witness, will you? He! he! he!

(53) *Tony.* Never fear me. Why! I'll say I saw them taken out with my own eyes.

(54) *Miss Nev.* I desire them but for a day, madam. Just to be permitted to show them as relics, and then they may be locked up again.

(55) *Mrs. Hard.* To be plain with you, my dear Constance, if I could find them you should have them. They're missing, I assure you. Lost, for aught I know; but we must have patience wherever they are.

(56) *Miss Nev.* I'll not believe it! this is but a shallow pretence to deny me. I know they are too valuable to be so slightly kept, and as you are to answer for the loss—

(57) *Mrs. Hard.* Don't be alarmed, Constance. If they be lost, I must restore an equivalent. But my son knows they are missing, and not to be found.

(58) *Tony.* That I can bear witness to. They are missing and not to be found; I'll take my oath on't.

(59) *Mrs. Hard.* You must learn resignation, my dear; for though we lose our fortune, yet we should not lose our patience. See me, how calm I am.

(60) *Miss Nev.* Ay, people are generally calm at the misfortunes of others.

(61) *Mrs. Hard.* Now I wonder a girl of your good sense should waste a thought upon such trumpery. We shall soon find them; and in the mean time you shall make use of my garnets till your jewels be found.

(62) *Miss Nev.* I detest garnets.

(63) *Mrs. Hard.* The most becoming things in the world to set off a clear complexion. You have often seen how well they look upon me. You *shall* have them.   [*Exit.*

(64) *Miss Nev.* I dislike them of all things. You sha'n't stir.—Was ever anything so provoking, to mislay my own jewels, and force me to wear her trumpery?

(65) *Tony.* Don't be a fool. If she gives you the garnets, take what you can get. The jewels are your own already. I have stolen them out of her bureau, and she does not know it. Fly to your spark, he'll tell you more of the matter. Leave me to manage her.

(66) *Miss Nev.* My dear cousin!

(67) *Tony.* Vanish. She's here, and has missed them already. [*Exit* Miss Neville.] See! how she fidgets and spits about like a Catherine wheel.

Enter Mrs. Hardcastle.

(68) *Mrs. Hard.* Confusion! thieves! robbers! we are cheated, plundered, broke open, undone.

(69) *Tony.* What's the matter, what's the matter, mamma? I hope nothing has happened to any of the good family!

(70) *Mrs. Hard.* We are robbed. My bureau has been broken open, the jewels taken out, and I'm undone.

(71) *Tony.* Oh! is that all? Ha! ha! ha! By the laws, I never saw it acted better in my life. Why, I thought you was ruined in earnest, ha! ha! ha!

(72) *Mrs. Hard.* Why, boy, I *am* ruined in earnest. My bureau has been broken open, and all taken away.

(73) *Tony.* Stick to that: ha! ha! ha! stick to that. I'll bear witness, you know; call me to bear witness.

(74) *Mrs. Hard.* I tell you, Tony, by all that's precious, the jewels are gone, and I shall be ruined for ever.

(75) *Tony.* Sure I know they are gone, and I'm to say so.

(76) *Mrs. Hard.* My dearest Tony, but hear me. They're gone, I say.

(77) *Tony.* By the laws, mamma, you make me for to laugh, ha! ha! I know who took them well enough, ha! ha! ha!

(78) *Mrs. Hard.* Was there ever such a blockhead, that can't tell the difference between jest and earnest? I tell you I'm not in jest, booby.

(79) *Tony.* That's right, that's right; you must be in a bitter passion, and then nobody will suspect either of us. I'll bear witness that they are gone.

(80) *Mrs. Hard.* Was there ever such a cross-grained brute, that won't hear me? Can you bear witness that you're no better than a fool? Was ever poor woman so beset with fools on one hand, and thieves on the other?

(81) *Tony.* I can bear witness to that.

(82) *Mrs. Hard.* Bear witness again, you blockhead you, and I'll turn you out of the room directly. My poor niece, what will become of her? Do you laugh, you unfeeling brute, as if you enjoyed my distress?

(83) *Tony.* I can bear witness to that.

(84) *Mrs. Hard.* Do you insult me, monster? I'll teach you to vex your mother, I will.

(85) *Tony.* I can bear witness to that.

[He runs off, she follows him.

Enter MISS HARDCASTLE *and* Maid.

(86) *Miss Hard.* What an unaccountable creature is that brother of mine, to send them to the house as an inn! ha! ha! I don't wonder at his impudence.

(87) *Maid.* But what is more, madam, the young gentleman, as you passed by in your present dress, asked me if you were the bar-maid. He mistook you for the bar-maid, madam.

(88) *Miss Hard.* Did he? Then as I live, I'm resolved to keep up the delusion. Tell me, Pimple, how do you like my present dress? Don't you think I look something like Cherry in the Beaux' Stratagem?

(89) *Maid.* It's the dress, madam, that every lady wears in the country, but when she visits or receives company.

(90) *Miss Hard.* And are you sure he does not remember my face or person?

(91) *Maid.* Certain of it.

(92) *Miss Hard.* I vow, I thought so; for, though we spoke for some time together, yet his fears were such, that he never once looked up during the interview. Indeed, if he had, my bonnet would have kept him from seeing me.

(93) *Maid.* But what do you hope from keeping him in his mistake?

(94) *Miss Hard.* In the first place I shall be seen, and that is no small advantage to a girl who brings her face to market. Then I shall perhaps make an acquaintance, and that's no small victory gained over one who never addresses any but the wildest of her sex. But my chief aim is, to take my gentleman off his guard, and, like an invisible champion of romance, examine the giant's force before I offer to combat.

(95) *Maid.* But are you sure you can act your part, and disguise your voice so that he may mistake that, as he has already mistaken your person?

(96) *Miss Hard.* Never fear me. I think I have got the true bar cant—Did your honour call?—Attend the Lion there —Pipes and tobacco for the angel.—The Lamb has been outrageous this half-hour.

(97) *Maid.* It will do, madam. But he's here. [*Exit* Maid.

Enter MARLOW.

(98) *Mar.* What a bawling in every part of the house! I have scarce a moment's repose. If I go to the best room, there I find my host and his story: if I fly to the gallery, there we have my hostess with her curtsey down to the ground. I have at last got a moment to myself, and now for recollection.   [*Walks and muses.*

(99) *Miss Hard.* Did you call, sir? Did your honour call?

(100) *Mar.* (*Musing.*) As for Miss Hardcastle, she's too grave and sentimental for me.

(101) *Miss Hard.* Did your honour call? (*She still places herself before him, he turning away.*)

(102) *Mar.* No, child. (*Musing.*) Besides, from the glimpse I had of her, I think she squints.

(103) *Miss Hard.* I'm sure, sir, I heard the bell ring.

(104) *Mar.* No, no. (*Musing.*) I have pleased my father, however, by coming down, and I'll to-morrow please myself by returning.   [*Taking out his tablets and perusing.*

(105) *Miss Hard.* Perhaps the other gentleman called, sir?

(106) *Mar.* I tell you, no.

(107) *Miss Hard.* I should be glad to know, sir. We have such a parcel of servants!

(108) *Mar.* No, no, I tell you. (*Looks full in her face.*) Yes, child, I think I did call. I wanted—I wanted—I vow, child, you are vastly handsome.

(109) *Miss Hard.* O la, sir, you'll make one ashamed.

(110) *Mar.* Never saw a more sprightly malicious eye. Yes, yes, my dear, I did call. Have you got any of your—a—what d'ye call it, in the house?

(111) *Miss Hard.* No, sir, we have been out of that these ten days.

(112) *Mar.* One may call in this house, I find, to very little purpose. Suppose I should call for a taste, just by way of a trial, of the nectar of your lips; perhaps I might be disappointed in that too.

(113) *Miss Hard.* Nectar! nectar! That's a liquor there's no call for in these parts. French, I suppose. We sell no French wines here, sir.

(114) *Mar.* Of true English growth, I assure you.

(115) *Miss Hard.* Then it's odd I should not know it. We brew all sort of wines in this house, and I have lived here these eighteen years.

(116) *Mar.* Eighteen years! Why, one would think, child, you kept the bar before you were born. How old are you?

(117) *Miss Hard.* O! sir, I must not tell my age. They say women and music should never be dated.

(118) *Mar.* To guess at this distance, you can't be much above forty (*approaching*). Yet, nearer, I don't think so much (*approaching*). By coming close to some women they look younger still; but when we come very close indeed—(*attempting to kiss her*).

(119) *Miss Hard.* Pray, sir, keep your distance. One would think you wanted to know one's age, as they do horses, by mark of mouth.

(120) *Mar.* I protest, child, you use me extremely ill. If you keep me at this distance, how is it possible you and I can ever be acquainted?

(121) *Miss Hard.* And who wants to be acquainted with you? I want no such acquaintance, not I. I'm sure you did not treat Miss Hardcastle, that was here awhile ago, in this obstropalous manner. I'll warrant me, before her you looked dashed, and kept bowing to the ground, and talked, for all the world, as if you was before a justice of peace.

(122) *Mar.* (*Aside.*) She has hit it, sure enough! (*To her.*) In awe of her, child? Ha! ha! ha! A mere awkward squinting thing; no, no. I find you don't know me. I laughed and rallied her a little; but I was unwilling to be too severe. No, I could not be too severe.

(123) *Miss Hard.* O! then, sir, you are a favourite, I find, among the ladies?

(124) *Mar.* Yes, my dear, a great favourite. And yet hang me, I don't see what they find in me to follow. At the Ladies' Club in town I'm called their agreeable Rattle. Rattle, child, is not my real name, but one I'm known by. My name is Solomons; Mr. Solomons, my dear, at your service. (*Offering to salute her.*)

(125) *Miss Hard.* Hold, sir; you are introducing me to your club, not to yourself. And you're so great a favourite there, you say?

(126) *Mar.* Yes, my dear. There's Mrs. Mantrap, Lady Betty Blackleg, the Countess of Sligo, Mrs. Langhorns, old Miss Biddy Buckskin, and your humble servant, keep up the spirit of the place.

(127) *Miss Hard.* Then it's a very merry place, I suppose?

(128) *Mar.* Yes, as merry as cards, supper, wine, and old women can make us.

(129) *Miss Hard.* And their agreeable Rattle, ha! ha! ha!

(130) *Mar.* (*Aside.*) I don't quite like this chit. She looks knowing, methinks. You laugh, child?

(131) *Miss Hard.* I can't but laugh, to think what time they all have for minding their work or their family.

(132) *Mar.* (*Aside.*) All's well; she don't laugh at me. (*To her.*) Do you ever work, child?

(133) *Miss Hard.* Ay, sure. There's not a screen or quilt in the whole house but what can bear witness to that.

(134) *Mar.* Indeed! then you must show me your embroidery. I embroider and draw patterns myself a little. If you want a judge of your work you must apply to me. (*Seizing her hand.*)

(135) *Miss Hard.* Ay, but the colours do not look well by candlelight. You shall see all in the morning. (*Struggling.*)

(136) *Mar.* And why not now, my angel? Such beauty fires beyond the power of resistance.—Pshaw! the father here! My old luck: I never nicked seven that I did not throw ames ace three times following.   [*Exit* MARLOW.

Enter HARDCASTLE, *who stands in surprise.*

(137) *Hard.* So, madam. So, I find *this* is your *modest* lover. This is your humble admirer, that kept his eyes fixed on the ground, and only adored at humble distance. Kate, Kate, art thou not ashamed to deceive your father so?

(138) *Miss Hard.* Never trust me, dear papa, but he's still the modest man I first took him for; you'll be convinced of it as well as I.

(139) *Hard.* By the hand of my body, I believe his impudence is infectious! Didn't I see him seize your hand? Didn't I see him haul you about like a milkmaid? And now you talk of his respect and his modesty, forsooth!

(140) *Miss Hard.* But if I shortly convince you of his modesty, that he has only the faults that will pass off with time, and the virtues that will improve with age, I hope you'll forgive him.

(141) *Hard.* The girl would actually make one run mad! I tell you, I'll not be convinced. I am convinced. He has scarce been three hours in the house, and he has already encroached on all my prerogatives. You may like his impudence, and call it modesty; but my son-in-law, madam, must have very different qualifications.

(142) *Miss Hard.* Sir, I ask but this night to convince you.

(143) *Hard.* You shall not have half the time, for I have thoughts of turning him out this very hour.

(144) *Miss Hard.* Give me that hour then, and I hope to satisfy you.

(145) *Hard.* Well, an hour let it be then. But I'll have no trifling with your father. All fair and open, do you mind me.

(146) *Miss Hard.* I hope, sir, you have ever found that I considered your commands as my pride; for your kindness is such, that my duty as yet has been inclination. [*Exeunt.*

ACT THE FOURTH.

SCENE—*The same.*

Enter HASTINGS *and* MISS NEVILLE.

(1) *Hast.* You surprise me; Sir Charles Marlow expected here this night! Where have you had your information?

(2) *Miss Nev.* You may depend upon it. I just saw his letter to Mr. Hardcastle, in which he tells him he intends setting out a few hours after his son.

(3) *Hast.* Then, my Constance, all must be completed before

he arrives. He knows me; and should he find me here, would discover my name, and perhaps my designs, to the rest of the family.

(4) *Miss Nev.* The jewels, I hope, are safe?

(5) *Hast.* Yes, yes, I have sent them to Marlow, who keeps the keys of our baggage. In the meantime, I'll go to prepare matters for our elopement. I have had the 'squire's promise of a fresh pair of horses; and if I should not see him again, will write him further directions. [*Exit.*

(6) *Miss Nev.* Well! success attend you. In the meantime I'll go and amuse my aunt with the old pretence of a violent passion for my cousin. [*Exit*

Enter MARLOW, *followed by a* Servant.

(7) *Mar.* I wonder what Hastings could mean by sending me so valuable a thing as a casket to keep for him, when he knows the only place I have is the seat of a post-coach at an inn-door. Have you deposited the casket with the landlady, as I ordered you? Have you put it into her own hands?

(8) *Ser.* Yes, your honour.

(9) *Mar.* She said she'd keep it safe, did she?

(10) *Ser.* Yes, she said she'd keep it safe enough; she asked me how I came by it; and she said she had a great mind to make me give an account of myself. [*Exit* Servant.

(11) *Mar.* Ha! ha! ha! They're safe, however. What an unaccountable set of beings have we got amongst! This little bar-maid though runs in my head most strangely, and drives out the absurdities of all the rest of the family. She's mine, she must be mine, or I'm greatly mistaken.

Enter HASTINGS.

(12) *Hast.* Bless me! I quite forgot to tell her that I intended to prepare at the bottom of the garden. Marlow here, and in spirits too!

(13) *Mar.* Give me joy, George. Crown me, shadow me with laurels! Well, George, after all, we modest fellows don't want for success among the women.

(14) *Hast.* Some women, you mean. But what success has

your honour's modesty been crowned with now, that it grows so insolent upon us?

(15) *Mar.* Didn't you see the tempting, brisk, lovely little thing, that runs about the house with a bunch of keys to its girdle?

(16) *Hast.* Well, and what then?

(17) *Mar.* She's mine, you rogue you. Such fire, such motion, such eyes, such lips; but 'faith! she would not let me kiss them though.

(18) *Hast.* But are you so sure, so very sure of her?

(19) *Mar.* Why, man, she talked of showing me her work above stairs, and I am to improve the pattern.

(20) *Hast.* But how can you, Charles, go about to rob a woman of her honour?

(21) *Mar.* Pshaw! pshaw! We all know the honour of the barmaid of an inn. I don't intend to rob her, take my word for it: there's nothing in this house I sha'n't honestly pay for.

(22) *Hast.* I believe the girl has virtue.

(23) *Mar.* And if she has, I should be the last man in the world that would attempt to corrupt it.

(24) *Hast.* You have taken care, I hope, of the casket I sent you to lock up? Is it in safety?

(25) *Mar.* Yes, yes. It's safe enough. I have taken care of it. But how could you think the seat of a post-coach at an inn-door a place of safety? Ah! numskull! I have taken better precautions for you than you did for yourself — I have—

(26) *Hast.* What?

(27) *Mar.* I have sent it to the landlady to keep for you.

(28) *Hast.* To the landlady!

(29) *Mar.* The landlady.

(30) *Hast.* You did?

(31) *Mar.* I did. She's to be answerable for its forthcoming, you know.

(32) *Hast.* Yes, she'll bring it forth with a witness.

(33) *Mar.* Wasn't I right? I believe you'll allow that I acted prudently upon this occasion.

(34) *Hast.* (*Aside.*) He must not see my uneasiness.

(35) *Mar.* You seem a little disconcerted though, methinks. Sure nothing has happened?

(36) *Hast.* No, nothing. Never was in better spirits in all my life. And so you left it with the landlady, who, no doubt, very readily undertook the charge.

(37) *Mar.* Rather too readily. For she not only kept the casket, but, through her great precaution, was going to keep the messenger too. Ha! ha! ha!

(38) *Hast.* He! he! he! They're safe, however.

(39) *Mar.* As a guinea in a miser's purse.

(40) *Hast.* (*Aside.*) So now all hopes of fortune are at an end, and we must set off without it. (*To him.*) Well, Charles, I'll leave you to your meditations on the pretty bar-maid, and, he! he! he! may you be as successful for yourself, as you have been for me!   [*Exit.*

(41) *Mar.* Thank ye, George: I ask no more. Ha! ha! ha!

Enter HARDCASTLE.

(42) *Hard.* I no longer know my own house. It's turned all topsy-turvy. His servants have got drunk already. I'll bear it no longer; and yet, from my respect for his father, I'll be calm. (*To him.*) Mr. Marlow, your servant. I'm your very humble servant. (*Bowing low.*)

(43) *Mar.* Sir, your humble servant. (*Aside.*) What's to be the wonder now?

(44) *Hard.* I believe, sir, you must be sensible, sir, that no man alive ought to be more welcome than your father's son, sir. I hope you think so?

(45) *Mar.* I do from my soul, sir. I don't want much en-treaty. I generally make my father's son welcome wherever he goes.

(46) *Hard.* I believe you do, from my soul, sir. But though I say nothing to your own conduct, that of your servants is insufferable. Their manner of drinking is setting a very bad example in this house, I assure you.

(47) *Mar.* I protest, my very good sir, that is no fault of mine. If they don't drink as they ought, they are to blame.

I ordered them not to spare the cellar. I did, I assure you. (*To the side scene.*) Here, let one of my servants come up. (*To him.*) My positive directions were, that as I did not drink myself, they should make up for my deficiencies below.

(48) *Hard.* Then they had your orders for what they do? I'm satisfied!

(49) *Mar.* They had, I assure you. You shall hear from one of themselves.

Enter Servant, *drunk.*

(50) *Mar.* You, Jeremy! Come forward, sirrah! What were my orders? Were you not told to drink freely, and call for what you thought fit, for the good of the house?

(51) *Hard.* (*Aside.*) I begin to lose my patience.

(52) *Jer.* Please your honour, liberty and Fleet Street for ever! Though I'm but a servant, I'm as good as another man. I'll drink for no man before supper, sir, hang me! Good liquor will sit upon a good supper, but a good supper will not sit upon—hiccup—on my conscience, sir.

(53) *Mar.* You see, my old friend, the fellow is as drunk as he can possibly be. I don't know what you'd have more, unless you'd have the poor wretch soused in a beer-barrel.

(54) *Hard.* He'll drive me distracted, if I contain myself any longer. Mr. Marlow—Sir; I have submitted to your insolence for more than four hours, and I see no likelihood of its coming to an end. I'm now resolved to be master here, sir; and I desire that you and your drunken pack may leave my house directly.

(55) *Mar.* Leave your house!—Sure you jest, my good friend! What? when I'm doing what I can to please you.

(56) *Hard.* I tell you, sir, you don't please me; so I desire you'll leave my house.

(57) *Mar.* Sure you cannot be serious? At this time o' night, and such a night? You only mean to banter me.

(58) *Hard.* I tell you, sir, I'm serious! and now that my passions are roused, I say this house is mine, sir; this house is mine, and I command you to leave it directly.

(59) *Mar.* Ha! ha! ha! A puddle in a storm. I sha'n't
stir a step, I assure you. (*In a serious tone.*) This your house,
fellow! It's my house. This is my house. Mine, while I
choose to stay. What right have you to bid me leave this
house, sir? I never met with such impudence, confound me;
never in my whole life before.

(60) *Hard.* Nor I, confound me if ever I did. To come to
my house, to call for what he likes, to turn me out of my own
chair, to insult the family, to order his servants to get drunk,
and then to tell me, "This house is mine, sir." By all that's
impudent, it makes me laugh. Ha! ha! ha! Pray, sir (*ban-
tering*), as you take the house, what think you of taking the
rest of the furniture? There's a pair of silver candlesticks,
and there's a fire-screen, and here's a pair of brazen-nozed bel-
lows; perhaps you may take a fancy to them?

(61) *Mar.* Bring me your bill, sir; bring me your bill, and
let's make no more words about it.

(62) *Hard.* There are a set of prints, too. What think you
of the Rake's Progress, for your own apartment?

(63) *Mar.* Bring me your bill, I say; and I'll leave you and
your infernal house directly.

(64) *Hard.* Then there's a mahogany table that you may
see your own face in.

(65) *Mar.* My bill, I say.

(66) *Hard.* I had forgot the great chair for your own particular slumbers, after a hearty meal.

(67) *Mar.* Bring me my bill, I say, and let's hear no
more on't.

(68) *Hard.* young man, young man, from your father's letter
to me, I was taught to expect a well-bred modest man as a
visitor here, but now I find him no better than a coxcomb
and a bully; but he will be down here presently, and shall
hear more of it. [*Exit.*

(69) *Mar.* How's this? Sure I have not mistaken the house.
Everything looks like an inn. The servants cry, coming; the
attendance is awkward; the barmaid, too, to attend us. But
she's here, and will further inform me. Whither so fast, child?
A word with you.

Enter MISS HARDCASTLE.

(70) *Miss Hard.* Let it be short, then. I'm in a hurry. (*Aside.*) I believe he begins to find out his mistake. But it's too soon quite to undeceive him.

(71) *Mar.* Pray, child, answer me one question. What are you, and what may your business in this house be?

(72) *Miss Hard.* A relation of the family, sir.

(73) *Mar.* What, a poor relation?

(74) *Miss Hard.* Yes, sir. A poor relation, appointed to keep the keys, and to see that the guests want nothing in my power to give them.

(75) *Mar.* That is, you act as the barmaid of this inn.

(76) *Miss Hard.* Inn! O law—what brought that in your head? One of the best families in the country keep an inn—Ha! ha! ha! old Mr. Hardcastle's house an inn!

(77) *Mar.* Mr. Hardcastle's house! Is this Mr. Hardcastle's house, child?

(78) *Miss Hard.* Ay, sure! Whose else should it be?

(79) *Mar.* So then, all's out, and I have been finely imposed on. O, confound my stupid head, I shall be laughed at over the whole town. I shall be stuck up in caricatura in all the print-shops. The *Dullissimo Maccaroni.* To mistake this house of all others for an inn, and my father's old friend for an innkeeper! What a swaggering puppy must he take me for! What a silly puppy do I find myself! There again, may I be hanged, my dear, but I mistook you for the barmaid.

(80) *Miss Hard.* Dear me! dear me! I'm sure there's nothing in my *behaviour* to put me on a level with one of that stamp.

(81) *Mar.* Nothing, my dear, nothing. But I was in for a list of blunders, and could not help making you a subscriber. My stupidity saw everything the wrong way. I mistook your assiduity for assurance, and your simplicity for allurement. But it's over. This house I no more show *my* face in.

(82) *Miss Hard.* I hope, sir, I have done nothing to disoblige you. I'm sure I should be sorry to affront any gentleman who has been so polite, and said so many civil things to me. I'm sure I should be sorry (*pretending to cry*) if he left

the family upon my account. I'm sure I should be sorry if people said anything amiss, since I have no fortune but my character.

(83) *Mar.* (*Aside.*) By heaven! she weeps. This is the first mark of tenderness I ever had from a modest woman, and it touches me. (*To her.*) Excuse me, my lovely girl; you are the only part of the family I leave with reluctance. But to be plain with you, the difference of our birth, fortune, and education, makes an honourable connection impossible; and I can never harbour a thought of seducing simplicity that trusted in my honour, of bringing ruin upon one whose only fault was being too lovely.

(84) *Miss Hard.* (*Aside.*) Generous man! I now begin to admire him. (*To him.*) But I am sure my family is as good as Miss Hardcastle's; and though I'm poor, that's no great misfortune to a contented mind; and, until this moment, I never thought that it was bad to want a fortune.

(85) *Mar.* And why now, my pretty simplicity?

(86) *Miss Hard.* Because it puts me at a distance from one that, if I had a thousand pounds, I would give it all to.

(87) *Mar.* (*Aside.*) This simplicity bewitches me, so that if I stay, I'm undone. I must make one bold effort and leave her. (*To her.*) Your partiality in my favour, my dear, touches me most sensibly: and were I to live for myself alone, I could easily fix my choice. But I owe too much to the opinion of the world, too much to the authority of a father; so that —I can scarcely speak it—it affects me. Farewell.   [*Exit.*

(88) *Miss Hard.* I never knew half his merit till now. He shall not go, if I have power or art to detain him. I'll still preserve the character in which I *stooped to conquer;* but will undeceive my papa, who perhaps may laugh him out of his resolution.   [*Exit.*

Enter TONY *and* MISS NEVILLE.

(89) *Tony.* Ay, you may steal for yourselves the next time. I have done my duty. She has got the jewels again, that's a sure thing; but she believes it was all a mistake of the servants.

(90) *Miss Nev.* But, my dear cousin, sure you won't forsake us in this distress? If she in the least suspects that I am going off, I shall certainly be locked up, or sent to my aunt Pedigree's, which is ten times worse.

(91) *Tony.* To be sure, aunts of all kinds are very bad things. But what can I do? I have got you a pair of horses that will fly like Whistle-jacket; and I'm sure you can't say but I have courted you nicely before her face. Here she comes, we must court a bit or two more, for fear she should suspect us.   [*They retire, and seem to fondle.*

Enter MRS. HARDCASTLE.

(92) *Mrs. Hard.* Well, I was greatly fluttered, to be sure. But my son tells me it was all a mistake of the servants. I sha'n't be easy, however, till they are fairly married, and then let her keep her own fortune. But what do I see? fondling together, as I'm alive. I never saw Tony so sprightly before. Ah! have I caught you, my pretty doves? What, billing, exchanging stolen glances and broken murmurs? Ah!

(93) *Tony.* As for murmurs, mother, we grumble a little now and then, to be sure. But there's no love lost between us.

(94) *Mrs. Hard.* A mere sprinkling, Tony, upon the flame, only to make it burn brighter.

(95) *Miss Nev.* Cousin Tony promises to give us more of his company at home. Indeed, he sha'n't leave us any more. It won't leave us, cousin Tony, will it?

(96) *Tony.* O! it's a pretty creature. No, I'd sooner leave my horse in a pound, than leave you when you smile upon one so. Your laugh makes you so becoming.

(97) *Miss Nev.* Agreeable cousin! Who can help admiring that natural humour, that pleasant, broad, red, thoughtless (*patting his cheek*)—ah! it's a bold face.

(98) *Mrs. Hard.* Pretty innocence!

(99) *Tony.* I'm sure I always loved cousin Con's hazle eyes, and her pretty long fingers, that she twists this way and that over the haspicholls, like a parcel of bobbins.

(100) *Mrs. Hard.* Ah! he would charm the bird from the tree. I was never so happy before. My boy takes after his

father, poor Mr. Lumpkin, exactly. The jewels, my dear Con, shall be yours incontinently. You shall have them. Isn't he a sweet boy, my dear? You shall be married to-morrow, and we'll put off the rest of his education, like Dr. Drowsy's sermons, to a fitter opportunity.

Enter DIGGORY.

(101) *Dig.* Where's the 'squire! I have got a letter for your worship.

(102) *Tony.* Give it to my mamma. She reads all my letters first.

(103) *Dig.* I had orders to deliver it into your own hands.

(104) *Tony.* Who does it come from?

(105) *Dig.* Your worship mun ask that o' the letter itself.

(106) *Tony.* I could wish to know though (*turning the letter, and gazing on it*).

(107) *Miss Nev.* (*Aside.*) Undone! undone! A letter to him from Hastings. I know the hand. If my aunt sees it, we are ruined for ever. I'll keep her employed a little if I can. (*To* MRS. HARDCASTLE.) But I have not told you, madam, of my cousin's smart answer just now to Mr. Marlow. We so laughed.—You must know, madam.—This way a little, for he must not hear us. [*They confer.*

(108) *Tony.* (*Still gazing.*) A confounded cramp piece of penmanship, as ever I saw in my life. I can read your print hand very well. But here are such handles, and shanks, and dashes, that one can scarce tell the head from the tail.—" To Anthony Lumpkin, Esquire." It's very odd, I can read the outside of my letters, where my own name is, well enough; but when I come to open it, it's all——buzz. That's hard, very hard; for the inside of the letter is always the cream of the correspondence.

(109) *Mrs. Hard.* Ha! ha! ha! Very well, very well. And so my son was too hard for the philosopher.

(110) *Miss Nev.* Yes, madam; but you must hear the rest, madam. A little more this way, or he may hear us. You'll hear how he puzzled him again.

(111) *Mrs. Hard.* He seems strangely puzzled now himself, methinks.

(112) *Tony.* (*Still gazing.*) A confounded up-and-down hand, as if it was disguised in liquor.—(*Reading.*) Dear sir,—ay, that's that. Then there's an M, and a T, and an S, but whether the next be an izzard, or an R, confound me, I cannot tell.

(113) *Mrs. Hard.* What's that, my dear? Can I give you any assistance?

(114) *Miss Nev.* Pray, aunt, let me read it. Nobody reads a cramp hand better than I. (*Twitching the letter from him.*) Do you know who it is from?

(115) *Tony.* Can't tell, except from Dick Ginger, the feeder.

(116) *Miss Nev.* Ay, so it is. (*Pretending to read.*) Dear 'Squire, hoping that you're in health, as I am at this present. The gentlemen of the Shake-bag club has cut the gentlemen of Goose-green quite out of feather. The odds—um—odd battle—um—long fighting—um—here, here, it's all about cocks and fighting; it's of no consequence; here, put it up, put it up. (*Thrusting the crumpled letter upon him.*)

(117) *Tony.* But I tell you, miss, it's of all the consequence in the world. I would not lose the rest of it for a guinea. Here, mother, do you make it out. Of no consequence! (*Giving* MRS. HARDCASTLE *the letter.*)

(118) *Mrs. Hard.* How's this?—(*Reads.*) " Dear 'Squire, I'm now waiting for Miss Neville, with a post-chaise and pair, at the bottom of the garden, but I find my horses yet unable to perform the journey. I expect you'll assist us with a pair of fresh horses, as you promised. Dispatch is necessary, as the *hag* (ay, the hag), your mother, will otherwise suspect us! Yours, Hastings." Grant me patience. I shall run distracted! My rage chokes me.

(119) *Miss Nev.* I hope, madam, you'll suspend your resentment for a few moments, and not impute to me any impertinence, or sinister design, that belongs to another.

(120) *Mrs. Hard.* (*Curtseying very low.*) Fine spoken, madam, you are most miraculously polite and engaging, and

quite the very pink of courtesy and circumspection, madam. (*Changing her tone.*) And you, you great ill-fashioned oaf, with scarce sense enough to keep your mouth shut: were you, too, joined against me? But I'll defeat all your plots in a moment. As for you, madam, since you have got a pair of fresh horses ready, it would be cruel to disappoint them. So, if you please, instead of running away with your spark, prepare, this very moment, to run off with *me*. Your old aunt Pedigree will keep you secure, I'll warrant me. You, too, sir, may mount your horse, and guard us upon the way. Here, Thomas, Roger, Diggory! I'll show you that I wish you better than you do yourselves.   [*Exit.*

(121) *Miss Nev.* So now I'm completely ruined.

(122) *Tony.* Ay, that's a sure thing.

(123) *Miss Nev.* What better could be expected from being connected with such a stupid fool,—and after all the nods and signs I made him?

(124) *Tony.* By the laws, miss, it was your own cleverness, and not my stupidity, that did your business. You were so nice and so busy with your Shake-bags and Goose-greens, that I thought you could never be making believe.

Enter HASTINGS.

(125) *Hast.* So, sir, I find by my servant, that you have shown my letter, and betrayed us. Was this well done, young gentleman?

(126) *Tony.* Here's another. Ask miss there, who betrayed you. It was her doing, not mine.

Enter MARLOW.

(127) *Mar.* So I have been finely used here among you. Rendered contemptible, driven into ill manners, despised, insulted, laughed at.

(128) *Tony.* Here's another. We shall have old Bedlam broke loose presently.

(129) *Miss Nev.* And there, sir, is the gentleman to whom we all owe every obligation.

(130) *Mar.* What can I say to him, a mere boy, an idiot, whose ignorance and age are a protection?

(131) *Hast.* A poor contemptible booby, that would but disgrace correction.

(132) *Miss Nev.* Yet with cunning and malice enough to make himself merry with all our embarrassments.

(133) *Hast.* An insensible cub.

(134) *Mar.* Replete with tricks and mischief.

(135) *Tony.* Baw! I'll fight you both, one after the other —with baskets.

(136) *Mar.* As for him, he's below resentment. But your conduct, Mr. Hastings, requires an explanation. You knew of my mistakes, yet would not undeceive me.

(137) *Hast.* Tortured as I am with my own disappointments, is this a time for explanations? It is not friendly, Mr. Marlow.

(138) *Mar.* But, sir—

(139) *Miss Nev.* Mr. Marlow, we never kept on your mistake till it was too late to undeceive you.

Enter Servant.

(140) *Ser.* My mistress desires you'll get ready immediately, madam. The horses are putting to. Your hat and things are in the next room. We are to go thirty miles before morning.   [*Exit* Servant.

(141) *Miss Nev.* Well, well: I'll come presently.

(142) *Mar.* (*To* HASTINGS.) Was it well done, sir, to assist in rendering me ridiculous? To hang me out for the scorn of all my acquaintance? Depend upon it, sir, I shall expect an explanation.

(143) *Hast.* Was it well done, sir, if you're upon that subject, to deliver what I intrusted to yourself, to the care of another, sir?

(144) *Miss Nev.* Mr. Hastings! Mr. Marlow! Why will you increase my distress by this groundless dispute? I implore, I entreat you—

Enter Servant.

(145) *Ser.* Your cloak, madam. My mistress is impatient.
                                          [*Exit* Servant.

(146) *Miss Nev.* I come. Pray be pacified. If I leave you thus, I shall die with apprehension.

Enter Servant.

(147) *Ser.* Your fan, muff, and gloves, madam. The horses are waiting.

(148) *Miss Nev.* O, Mr. Marlow! if you knew what a scene of constraint and ill-nature lies before me, I'm sure it would convert your resentment into pity.

(149) *Mar.* I'm so distracted with a variety of passions, that I don't know what I do. Forgive me, madam. George, forgive me. You know my hasty temper, and should not exasperate it.

(150) *Hast.* The torture of my situation is my only excuse.

(151) *Miss Nev.* Well, my dear Hastings, if you have that esteem for me that I think, that I am sure you have, your constancy for three years will but increase the happiness of our future connection. If—

(152) *Mrs. Hard.* (*Within.*) Miss Neville. Constance, why Constance, I say.

(153) *Miss Nev.* I'm coming. Well, constancy, remember, constancy is the word.   [*Exit.*

(154) *Hast.* My heart! how can I support this? To be so near happiness, and such happiness!

(155) *Mar.* (*To* Tony.) You see now, young gentleman, the effects of your folly. What might be amusement to you, is here disappointment, and even distress.

(156) *Tony.* (*From a reverie.*) Stop, I have hit it. It's here. Your hands. Yours and yours, my poor Sulky!—My boots there, ho!—Meet me two hours hence at the bottom of the garden; and if you don't find Tony Lumpkin a more good-natured fellow than you thought for, I'll give you leave to take my best horse, and Bet Bouncer into the bargain. Come along. My boots, ho!   [*Exeunt.*

ACT THE FIFTH.

Scene I.—*The same.*

Enter Hastings *and* Servant.

(1) *Hast.* You saw the old lady and Miss Neville drive off, you say?

(2) *Ser.* Yes, your honour. They went off in a post-coach, and the young 'squire went on horseback. They're thirty miles off by this time.

(3) *Hast.* Then all my hopes are over.

(4) *Ser.* Yes, sir. Old Sir Charles has arrived. He and the old gentleman of the house have been laughing at Mr. Marlow's mistake this half hour. They are coming this way.

(5) *Hast.* Then I must not be seen. So now to my fruitless appointment at the bottom of the garden. This is about the time.   [*Exit.*

Enter Sir Charles *and* Hardcastle.

(6) *Hard.* Ha! ha! ha! The peremptory tone in which he sent forth his sublime commands!

(7) *Sir Cha.* And the reserve with which I suppose he retated all your advances.

(8) *Hard.* And yet he might have seen something in me above a common innkeeper, too.

(9) *Sir Cha.* Yes, Dick, but he mistook you for an uncommon innkeeper, ha! ha! ha!

(10) *Hard.* Well, I'm in too good spirits to think of anything but joy. Yes, my dear friend, this union of our families will make our personal friendships hereditary; and though my daughter's fortune is but small—

(11) *Sir Cha.* Why, Dick, will you talk of fortune to *me?* My son is possessed of more than a competence already, and can want nothing but a good and virtuous girl to share his happiness and increase it. If they like each other, as you say they do—

(12) *Hard. If*, man! I tell you they *do* like each other. My daughter as good as told me so.

(13) *Sir Cha.* But girls are apt to flatter themselves, you know.

(14) *Hard.* I saw him grasp her hand in the warmest manner myself: and here he comes to put you out of your *ifs*, I warrant him.

Enter MARLOW.

(15) *Mar.* I come, sir, once more, to ask pardon for my strange conduct. I can scarce reflect on my insolence without confusion.

(16) *Hard.* Tut, boy, a trifle! You take it too gravely. An hour or two's laughing with my daughter will set all to rights again. She'll never like you the worse for it.

(17) *Mar.* Sir, I shall be always proud of her approbation.

(18) *Hard.* Approbation is but a cold word, Mr. Marlow; if I am not deceived, you have something more than approbation thereabouts. You take me?

(19) *Mar.* Really, sir, I have not that happiness.

(20) *Hard.* Come, boy, I'm an old fellow, and know what's what as well as you that are younger. I know what has passed between you; but mum.

(21) *Mar.* Sure, sir, nothing has passed between us but the most profound respect on my side, and the most distant reserve on hers. You don't think, sir, that my impudence has been passed upon all the rest of the family.

(22) *Hard.* Impudence! No, I don't say that—not quite impudence—though girls like to be played with, and rumpled a little too, sometimes. But she has told no tales, I assure you.

(23) *Mar.* I never gave her the slightest cause.

(24) *Hard.* Well, well, I like modesty in its place well enough. But this is over-acting, young gentleman. You may be open. Your father and I will like you all the better for it.

(25) *Mar.* May I die, sir, if I ever—

(26) *Hard.* I tell you, she don't dislike you; and as I'm sure you like her—

(27) *Mar.* Dear sir—I protest, sir—

(28) *Hard.* I see no reason why you should not be joined as fast as the parson can tie you.

(29) *Mar.* But hear me, sir—

(30) *Hard.* Your father approves the match, I admire it; every moment's delay will be doing mischief. So—

(31) *Mar.* But why won't you hear me? By all that's just and true, I never gave Miss Hardcastle the slightest mark of my attachment, or even the most distant hint to suspect me off affection. We had but one interview, and that was formal, modest, and uninteresting.

(32) *Hard.* (*Aside.*) This fellow's formal modest impudence is beyond bearing.

(33) *Sir Cha.* And you never grasped her hand, or made any protestations?

(34) *Mar.* As Heaven is my witness, I came down in obedience to your commands. I saw the lady without emotion, and parted without reluctance. I hope you'll exact no further proofs of my duty, nor prevent me from leaving a house in which I suffer so many mortifications.   [*Exit.*

(35) *Sir Cha.* I'm astonished at the air of sincerity with which he parted.

(36) *Hard.* And I'm astonished at the deliberate intrepidity of his assurance.

(37) *Sir Cha.* I dare pledge my life and honour upon his truth.

(38) *Hard.* Here comes my daughter, and I would stake my happiness upon her veracity.

Enter MISS HARDCASTLE.

(39) *Hard.* Kate, come hither, child. Answer us sincerely and without reserve; has Mr. Marlow made you any professions of love and affection?

(40) *Miss Hard.* The question is very abrupt, sir. But since you require unreserved sincerity, I think he has.

(41) *Hard.* (*To* SIR CHARLES.) You see.

(42) *Sir Cha.* And pray, madam, have you and my son had more than one interview?

(43) *Miss Hard.* Yes, sir, several.

(44) *Hard.* (*To* SIR CHARLES.) You see.

(45) *Sir Cha.* But did he profess any attachment?

(46) *Miss Hard.* A lasting one.

(47) *Sir Cha.* Did he talk of love?

(48) *Miss Hard.* Much, sir.

(49) *Sir Cha.* Amazing! And all this formally.

(50) *Miss Hard.* Formally.

(51) *Hard.* Now, my friend, I hope you are satisfied.

(52) *Sir Cha.* And how did he behave, madam?

(53) *Miss Hard.* As most profest admirers do: said some civil things of my face, talked much of his want of merit, and the greatness of mine; mentioned his heart, gave a short tragedy speech, and ended with pretended rapture.

(54) *Sir Cha.* Now I'm perfectly convinced, indeed. I know his conversation among women to be modest and submissive: this forward canting ranting manner by no means describes him; and, I am confident, he never sat for the picture.

(55) *Miss Hard.* Then, what, sir, if I should convince you to your face of my sincerity? If you and my papa, in about half an hour, will place yourselves behind that screen, you shall hear him declare his passion to me in person.

(56) *Sir Cha.* Agreed. And if I find him what you describe, all my happiness in him must have an end.   [*Exit.*

(57) *Miss Hard.* And if you don't find him what I describe —I fear my happiness must never have a beginning. [*Exeunt.*

SCENE II.—*The back of the Garden.*

Enter HASTINGS.

(1) *Hast.* What an idiot am I, to wait here for a fellow who probably takes a delight in mortifying me. He never intended to be punctual, and I'll wait no longer. What do I see? It is he! and perhaps with news of my Constance.

Enter TONY, *booted and spattered.*

(2) *Hast.* My honest 'squire! I now find you a man of your word. This looks like friendship.

(3) *Tony.* Ay, I'm your friend, and the best friend you have in the world, if you knew but all. This riding by night, by the bye, is cursedly tiresome. It has shook me worse than the basket of a stage-coach.

(4) *Hast.* But how? where did you leave your fellow-travellers? Are they in safety? Are they housed?

(5) *Tony.* Five and twenty miles in two hours and a half is no such bad driving. The poor beasts have smoked for it: rabbit me, but I'd rather ride forty miles after a fox than ten with such varment.

(6) *Hast.* Well, but where have you left the ladies? I die with impatience.

(7) *Tony.* Left them! Why, where should I leave them but where I found them?

(8) *Hast.* This is a riddle.

(9) *Tony.* Riddle me this then. What's that goes round the house, and round the house, and never touches the house?

(10) *Hast.* I'm still astray.

(11) *Tony.* Why, that's it, mon. I have led them astray. By jingo, there's not a pond or a slough within five miles of the place but they can tell the taste of.

(12) *Hast.* Ha! ha! ha! I understand: you took them in a round, while they supposed themselves going forward, and so you have at last brought them home again.

(13) *Tony.* You shall hear. I first took them down Feather-bed Lane, where we stuck fast in the mud. I then rattled them crack over the stones of Up-and-down Hill. I then introduced them to the gibbet on Heavy-tree Heath; and from that, with a circumbendibus, I fairly lodged them in the horse-pond at the bottom of the garden.

(14) *Hast.* But no accident, I hope?

(15) *Tony.* No, no. Only mother is confoundedly frightened. She thinks herself forty miles off. She's sick of the journey; and the cattle can scarce crawl. So if your own horses be ready, you may whip off with cousin, and I'll be bound that no soul here can budge a foot to follow you.

(16) *Hast.* My dear friend, how can I be grateful?

(17) *Tony.* Ay, now it's dear friend, noble 'squire. Just

now, it was all idiot, cub, and run me through the guts. Hang *your* way of fighting, I say. After we take a knock in this part of the country, we kiss and be friends. But if you had run me through the guts, then I should be dead, and you might go kiss the hangman.

(18) *Hast.* The rebuke is just. But I must hasten to relieve Miss Neville: if you keep the old lady employed, I promise to take care of the young one.   [*Exit* HASTINGS.

(19) *Tony.* Never fear me. Here she comes. Vanish. She's got from the pond, and draggled up to the waist like a mermaid.

Enter MRS. HARDCASTLE.

(20) *Mrs. Hard.* Oh, Tony, I'm killed! Shook! Battered to death. I shall never survive it. That last jolt, that laid us against the quickset hedge, has done my business.

(21) *Tony.* Alack, mamma, it was all your own fault. You would be for running away by night, without knowing one inch of the way.

(22) *Mrs. Hard.* I wish we were at home again. I never met so many accidents in so short a journey. Drenched in the mud, overturned in a ditch, stuck fast in a slough, jolted to a jelly, and at last to lose our way. Whereabouts do you think we are, Tony?

(23) *Tony.* By my guess we should come upon Crackskull common, about forty miles from home.

(24) *Mrs. Hard.* O dear! O dear! The most notorious spot in all the country. We only want a robbery to make a complete night on't.

(25) *Tony.* Don't be afraid, mamma, don't be afraid. Two of the five that kept here are hanged, and the other three may not find us. Don't be afraid.—Is that a man that's galloping behind us? No! it's only a tree.—Don't be afraid.

(26) *Mrs. Hard.* The fright will certainly kill me.

(27) *Tony.* Do you see anything like a black hat moving behind the thicket?

(28) *Mrs. Hard.* Oh, death!

(29) *Tony.* No; it's only a cow. Don't be afraid, mamma; don't be afraid.

(30) *Mrs. Hard.* As I'm alive, Tony, I see a man coming towards us. Ah! I'm sure on't. If he perceives us, we are undone.

(31) *Tony.* (*Aside.*) Father-in-law, by all that's unlucky, come to take one of his night walks. (*To her.*) Ah! it's a high-wayman with pistols as long as my arm. A most ill-looking fellow.

(32) *Mrs. Hard.* Good Heaven defend us! He approaches.

(33) *Tony.* Do you hide yourself in that thicket, and leave me to manage him. If there be any danger, I'll cough, and cry hem. When I cough, be sure to keep close. (Mrs. Hardcastle *hides behind a tree in the back scene.*)

Enter HARDCASTLE.

(34) *Hard.* I'm mistaken, or I heard voices of people in want of help. Oh, Tony! is that you? I did not expect you so soon back. Are your mother and her charge in safety?

(35) *Tony.* Very safe, sir, at my aunt Pedigree's. Hem!

(36) *Mrs. Hard.* (*From behind.*) Ah, death! I find there's danger.

(37) *Hard.* Forty miles in three hours; sure that's too much, my youngster.

(38) *Tony.* Stout horses and willing minds make short journeys, as they say. Hem!

(39) *Mrs. Hard.* (*From behind.*) Sure he'll do the dear boy no harm.

(40) *Hard.* But I heard a voice here; I should be glad to know from whence it came.

(41) *Tony.* It was I, sir, talking to myself, sir. I was saying that forty miles in four hours was very good going. Hem! As to be sure it was. Hem! I have got a sort of cold by being out in the air. We'll go in, if you please. Hem!

(42) *Hard.* But if you talked to yourself you did not answer yourself. I'm certain I heard two voices, and am resolved (*raising his voice*) to find the other out.

(43) *Mrs. Hard.* (*From behind.*) Oh! he's coming to find me out. Oh!

(44) *Tony.* What need you go, sir, if I tell you? Hem! I'll lay down my life for the truth—hem!—I'll tell you all, sir.
[*Detaining him.*

(45) *Hard.* I tell you I will not be detained. I insist on seeing. It's in vain to expect I'll believe you.

(46) *Mrs. Hard.* (*Running forward from behind.*) O dear! he'll murder my poor boy, my darling! Here, good gentleman, whet your rage upon me. Take my money, my life, but spare that young gentleman; spare my child, if you have any mercy.

(47) *Hard.* My wife, as I'm a Christian. From whence can she come? or what does she mean?

(48) *Mrs. Hard.* (*Kneeling.*) Take compassion on us, good Mr. Highwayman. Take our money, our watches, all we have, but spare our lives. We will never bring you to justice; indeed we won't, good Mr. Highwayman.

(49) *Hard.* I believe the woman's out of her senses. What, Dorothy, don't you know *me?*

(50) *Mrs. Hard.* Mr. Hardcastle, as I'm alive. My fears blinded me. But who, my dear, could have expected to meet you here, in this frightful place, so far from home? What has brought you to follow us?

(51) *Hard.* Sure, Dorothy, you have not lost your wits? So far from home, when you are within forty yards of your own door! (*To him.*) This is one of your old tricks, you graceless rogue, you. (*To her.*) Don't you know the gate, and the mulberry-tree; and don't you remember the horse-pond, my dear?

(52) *Mrs. Hard.* Yes, I shall remember the horse-pond as long as I live; I have caught my death in it. (*To* TONY.) And is it to you, you graceless varlet, I owe all this? I'll teach you to abuse your mother, I will.

(53) *Tony.* Well, mother, all the parish says you have spoiled me, and so you may take the fruits on't.

(54) *Mrs. Hard.* I'll spoil you, I will.
[*Follows him off the stage. Exit,*

(55) *Hard.* There's morality, however, in his reply. [*Exit*

Enter HASTINGS *and* MISS NEVILLE.

(56) *Hast.* My dear Constance, why will you deliberate thus? If we delay a moment, all is lost for ever. Pluck up a little resolution, and we shall soon be out of the reach of her malignity.

(57) *Miss Nev.* I find it impossible. My spirits are so sunk with the agitations I have suffered, that I am unable to face any new danger. Two or three years' patience will at last crown us with happiness.

(58) *Hast.* Such a tedious delay is worse than inconstancy. Let us fly, my charmer. Let us date our happiness from this very moment. Perish fortune! Love and content will increase what we possess beyond a monarch's revenue. Let me prevail!

(59) *Miss Nev.* No, Mr. Hastings, no. Prudence once more comes to my relief, and I will obey its dictates. In the moment of passion fortune may be despised, but it ever produces a lasting repentance. I'm resolved to apply to Mr. Hardcastle's compassion and justice for redress.

(60) *Hast.* But though he had the will, he has not the power to relieve you.

(61) *Miss Nev.* But he has influence, and upon that I am resolved to rely.

(62) *Hast.* I have no hopes. But since you persist, I must reluctantly obey you.   [*Exeunt.*

SCENE III., *as in Scene I.*

Enter SIR CHARLES *and* MISS HARDCASTLE.

(1) *Sir Cha.* What a situation am I in! If what you say appears, I shall then find a guilty son. If what he says be true, I shall then lose one that, of all others, I most wished for a daughter.

(2) *Miss Hard.* I am proud of your approbation, and to show I merit it, if you place yourselves as I directed, you shall hear his explicit declaration. But he comes.

(3) *Sir Cha.* I'll to your father, and keep him to the appointment.   [*Exit* Sir Charles.

Enter MARLOW.

(4) *Mar.* Though prepared for setting out, I come once more to take leave; nor did I, till this moment, know the pain I feel in the separation.

(5) *Miss Hard.* (*In her own natural manner.*) I believe these sufferings cannot be very great, sir, which you can so easily remove. A day or two longer, perhaps, might lessen your uneasiness, by showing the little value of what you now think proper to regret.

(6) *Mar.* (*Aside.*) This girl every moment improves upon me. (*To her.*) It must not be, madam. I have already trifled too long with my heart. My very pride begins to submit to my passion. The disparity of education and fortune, the anger of a parent, and the contempt of my equals, begin to lose their weight; and nothing can restore me to myself but this painful effort of resolution.

(7) *Miss Hard.* Then go, sir: I'll urge nothing more to detain you. Though my family be as good as hers you came down to visit, and my education, I hope, not inferior, what are these advantages without equal affluence? I must remain contented with the slight approbation of imputed merit; I must have only the mockery of your addresses, while all your serious aims are fixed on fortune.

Enter HARDCASTLE *and* SIR CHARLES *from behind.*

(8) *Sir Char.* Here, behind this screen.

(9) *Hard.* Ay, ay, make no noise. I'll engage my Kate covers him with confusion at last.

(10) *Mar.* By heavens, madam! fortune was ever my smallest consideration. Your beauty at first caught my eye; for who could see that without emotion? But every moment that I converse with you steals in some new grace, heightens the picture, and gives it stronger expression. What at first seemed rustic plainness, now appears refined simplicity. What seemed forward assurance, now strikes me as the result of courageous innocence and conscious virtue.

(11) *Sir Cha.* What can it mean? He amazes me!

(12) *Hard.* I told you how it would be. Hush!

(13) *Mar.* I am now determined to stay, madam; and I have too good an opinion of my father's discernment, when he sees you, to doubt his approbation.

(14) *Miss Hard.* No, Mr. Marlow, I will not, cannot detain you. Do you think I could suffer a connection in which there is the smallest room for repentance? Do you think I would take the mean advantage of a transient passion, to load you with confusion? Do you think I could ever relish that happiness which was acquired by lessening yours?

(15) *Mar.* By all that's good, I can have no happiness but what's in your power to grant me! Nor shall I ever feel repentance but in not having seen your merits before. I will stay even contrary to your wishes; and though you should persist to shun me, I will make my respectful assiduities atone for the levity of my past conduct.

(16) *Miss Hard.* Sir, I must entreat you'll desist. As our acquaintance began, so let it end, in indifference. I might have given an hour or two to levity; but seriously, Mr. Marlow, do you think I could ever submit to a connection where I must appear mercenary, and you imprudent? Do you think I could ever catch at the confident addresses of a secure admirer?

(17) *Mar.* (*Kneeling.*) Does this look like security? Does this look like confidence? No, madam, every moment that shows me your merit, only serves to increase my diffidence and confusion. Here let me continue—

(18) *Sir Cha.* I can hold it no longer. Charles, Charles, how hast thou deceived me! Is this your indifference, your uninteresting conversation?

(19) *Hard.* Your cold contempt; your formal interview! What have you to say now?

(20) *Mar.* That I'm all amazement! What can it mean?

(21) *Hard.* It means that you can say and unsay things at pleasure: that you can address a lady in private, and deny it in public: that you have one story for us, and another for my daughter.

(22) *Mar.* Daughter!—this lady your daughter?

(23) *Hard.* Yes, sir, my only daughter; my Kate; whose else should she be?

(24) *Mar.* Oh, the mischief!

(25) *Miss Hard.* Yes, sir, that very identical tall squinting lady you were pleased to take me for (*courtseying*); she that you addressed as the mild, modest, sentimental man of gravity, and the bold, forward agreeable Rattle of the Ladies' Club. Ha! ha! ha!

(26) *Mar.* What! there's no bearing this; it's worse than death!

(27) *Miss Hard.* In which of your characters, sir, will you give us leave to address you? As the faltering gentleman, with looks on the ground, that speaks just to be heard, and hates hypocrisy; or the loud confident creature, that keeps it up with Mrs. Mantrap, and old Miss Biddy Buckskin, till three in the morning? Ha! ha! ha!

(28) *Mar.* O, curse on my noisy head. I never attempted to be impudent yet, that I was not taken down. I must be gone.

(29) *Hard.* By the hand of my body, but you shall not. I see it was all a mistake, and I am rejoiced to find it. You shall not, sir, I tell you. I know she'll forgive you. Won't you forgive him, Kate? We'll all forgive you. Take courage, man. (*They retire, she tormenting him, to the back scene.*)

Enter MRS. HARDCASTLE *and* TONY.

(30) *Mrs. Hard.* So, so, they're gone off. Let them go, I care not.

(31) *Hard.* Who gone?

(32) *Mrs. Hard.* My dutiful niece and her gentleman, Mr. Hastings, from town. He who came down with our modest visitor here.

(33) *Sir Cha.* Who, my honest George Hastings? As worthy a fellow as lives, and the girl could not have made a more prudent choice.

(34) *Hard.* Then, by the hand of my body, I'm proud of the connection.

(35) *Mrs. Hard.* Well, if he has taken away the lady, he

has not taken her fortune; that remains in the family to con-
sole us for her loss.

(36) *Hard.* Sure, Dorothy, you would not be so mercenary?

(37) *Mrs. Hard.* Ay, that's my affair, not yours.

(38) *Hard.* But you know if your son, when of age, refuses
to marry his cousin, her whole fortune is then at her own
disposal.

(39) *Mrs. Hard.* Ay, but he's not of age, and she has not
thought proper to wait for his refusal.

Enter HASTINGS *and* MISS NEVILLE.

(40) *Mrs. Hard.* (*Aside.*) What, returned so soon! I begin
not to like it.

(41) *Hast.* (*To* HARDCASTLE.) For my late attempt to fly
off with your niece let my present confusion be my punish-
ment. We are now come back, to appeal from your justice to
your humanity. By her father's consent I first paid her my
addresses, and our passions were first founded in duty.

(42) *Miss Nev.* Since his death, I have been obliged to
stoop to dissimulation to avoid oppression. In an hour of
levity I was ready to give up my fortune to secure my choice.
But I am now recovered from the delusion, and hope from
your tenderness what is denied me from a nearer connection.

(43) *Mrs. Hard.* Pshaw, pshaw! this is all but the whining
end of a modern novel.

(44) *Hard.* Be it what it will, I'm glad they're come back
to reclaim their due. Come hither, Tony, boy. Do you
refuse this lady's hand whom I now offer you?

(45) *Tony.* What signifies my refusing? You know I can't
refuse her till I'm of age, father.

(46) *Hard.* While I thought concealing your age, boy, was
likely to conduce to your improvement, I concurred with your
mother's desire to keep it secret. But since I find she turns
it to a wrong use, I must now declare you have been of age
these three months.

(47) *Tony.* Of age! Am I of age, father?

(48) *Hard.* Above three months.

(49) *Tony.* Then you'll see the first use I'll make of my

liberty. (*Taking* MISS NEVILLE's *hand.*) Witness all men by these presents, that I, Anthony Lumpkin, Esquire, of BLANK place, refuse you, Constantia Neville, spinster, of no place at all, for my true and lawful wife. So Constance Neville may marry whom she pleases, and Tony Lumpkin is his own man again.

(50) *Sir Cha.* O brave 'squire!

(51) *Hast.* My worthy friend!

(52) *Mrs. Hard.* My undutiful offspring!

(53) *Mar.* Joy, my dear George! I give you joy sincerely. And could I prevail upon my little tyrant here to be less arbitrary, I should be the happiest man alive, if you would return me the favour.

(54) *Hast.* (*To* MISS HARDCASTLE.) Come, madam, you are now driven to the very last scene of all your contrivances. I know you like him, I'm sure he loves you, and you must and shall have him.

(55) *Hard.* (*Joining their hands.*) And I say so too. And, Mr. Marlow, if she makes as good a wife as she has a daughter, I don't believe you'll ever repent your bargain. So now to supper. To-morrow we shall gather all the poor of the parish about us, and the mistakes of the night shall be crowned with a merry morning. So, boy, take her; and as you have been mistaken in the mistress, my wish is, that you may never be mistaken in the wife.   [*Exeunt Omnes.*

EPILOGUE.

SPOKEN BY MRS. BULKLEY, AS MISS HARDCASTLE.

Well, having stoop'd to conquer with success,
And gain'd a husband without aid from dress:
Still as a barmaid, I could wish it too
As I have conquered him to conquer you: (4)
And let me say, for all your resolution,
That pretty barmaids have done execution.
Our life is all a play, compos'd to please,
" We have our exits and our entrances."   (8)

The first act shows the simple country maid,
Harmless and young, of everything afraid;
Blushes when hir'd, and with unmeaning action,
"I hope as how to give you satisfaction."   (12)
Her second act displays a livelier scene—
Th' unblushing barmaid of a country-inn,
Who whisks about the house, at market caters,
Talks loud, coquets the guests, and scolds the waiters. (16)
Next the scene shifts to town, and there she soars,
The chop-house toast of ogling *connoisseurs*.
On squires and cits she there displays her arts,
And on the gridiron broils her lovers' hearts—   (20)
And as she smiles, her triumphs to complete,
E'en common-councilmen forget to eat.
The fourth act shows her wedded to the squire,
And madam now begins to hold it higher;   (24)
Pretends to taste, at operas cries caro,
And quits her Nancy Dawson for Che Faro:
Doats upon dancing, and in all her pride
Swims round the room, the Heinel of Cheapside: (28)
Ogles and leers with artificial skill,
Till having lost in age the power to kill,
She sits all night at cards, and ogles at spadille.
Such, through our lives the eventful history—   (32)
The fifth and last act still remains for me.
The barmaid now for your protection prays,
Turns female Barrister, and pleads for Bays.

NOTES

TO "SHE STOOPS TO CONQUER."

PROLOGUE.

The Prologue was written by Garrick, for a good account of whom see Daniel's *Merrie England in the Olden Time*, pp. 233-235. Woodward, the actor who spoke this prologue, had refused the part of Tony Lumpkin before it was offered to Quick. The prologue satirizes the sentimental school that was killing true comedy.

(3) **'Tis not alone.** See *Hamlet* i. i. 77-86: "'Tis not alone my inky cloak, good mother."

(6) **The comic muse.** Thalia. A more serious lament for comedy will be found in Spenser's *Teares of the Muses*.

(7, 8) If she (comedy) dies, I shall never cease to mourn, because I am, as a player, unable to weep (play tragic parts).

(11) **the sweet maid,** true comedy.

(12) **Ned Shuter,** the actor who had played the part of Croaker so successfully. He and Woodward were two of the best comic actors of their day.

(13) **drab,** sentimental comedy. **mawkish,** squeamish: [from old Eng *mawl*, a maggot; thence, loathsome]. **drab,** a slut [Keltic].

(15) **to all intents,** or to all intents and purposes, *i.e.* practically, for all practical purposes we are as useless as if dead.

(20) **They,** the managers of the theatre.

(22) **fixed,** perf. partic. absolute: my face and eye being fixed, rigid, unchanging.

(25-30) a parody of the sententious moralizings of the new and fashionable sentimental comedies.

(31) **I give it up,** I give up the attempt to be "moral" (*i.e.* to moralize).

(32) cf. line 8, tragedy, as played by him, would be ludicrous.

(34) **A Doctor,** Oliver Goldsmith, M.B. but not M.D., and therefore only "Doctor" by courtesy.

(35) **muscles** of the face moved by laughter.

(36) **Draughts,** doses, *i.e.* Acts of the Play.

(38) **Swallow,** in its colloquial sense of tolerate, endure.

(39) her case and the Doctor *is* desperate; false concord for sake of rhyme.

(42) **No poisonous drugs,** nothing contrary to decency and morality.

(44) **within,** from the theatre, the people inside or behind the scenes.

(45) **The College of Physicians,** who had the right of conferring diplomas. *you* in apposition to *college*.

(46) **Regular,** a licensed practitioner, a successful playwright; **quack,** a mountebank, an impostor.

DRAMATIS PERSONÆ.

Persons of the drama. **Sir Charles Marlow,** friend of Hardcastle. **Young Marlow,** his son, come to woo Hardcastle's daughter. **Hardcastle,** an old country gentleman. **Hastings,** friend of young Marlow, and in love with Miss Neville, Mrs. Hardcastle's niece and ward. **Tony Lumpkin**, son of Mrs. Hardcastle by her first husband. **Diggory**, a farm-servant. **Mrs. Hardcastle**, wife of Hardcastle. **Miss Hardcastle**, daughter of Mr. and Mrs. H., wooed by young Marlow under the idea that she is a poor relation of the Hardcastles. **Miss Neville**, an orphan, cousin of Miss Hardcastle, and under Mrs. Hardcastle's guardianship. Wooed by Mrs. H. for Tony, in order to keep her jewels in the family; but secretly engaged to Hastings. **Maid**, attending on Miss Hardcastle. **Stingo**, the **Landlord** of the Three Jolly Pigeons Inn, &c. &c.

ACT I.—Scene 1.

Speech (1) For convenience of reference to other editions, as the dialogue is in prose, the speeches and not the lines have been numbered. **particular**, odd, peculiar. **a trip**, a journey, an excursion. **rub off the rust**, civilize, polish ourselves (note that *polish* and *polite* come from Lat. *polire*, and have *nothing* to do with Greek *polis*, a city).

(2) **in my time**, when I was young. **the very basket**, in old stage-coaches the two outside seats facing each other behind were called the *basket*.

(3) **rumbling**, dilapidated. **for all the world** exactly **like an inn**: this helps the audience to admit the probability of the chief mistake on which the plot turns. **company**, guests, visitors. **Cripplegate**, suggestive of **cripplegait**, an appropriate name for a lame man. There is a place called Cripplegate in London [cripple, literally one who creeps; the suffix has the same active force as in A.-S. *bȳd-el*, *i.e.* one who proclaims, a beadle. Skeat]. **Prince Eugene**, François Eugene, prince of Savoy, and commander in the Austrian army, 1663–1736. John Churchill, first **Duke of Marlborough**, English general and statesman, 1650–1722. See Bright's *Hist. of England*, and for a fuller account Burton's *Reign of Queen Anne*. **deceit**, Fr. *tromperie*, from *tromper*, to deceive; *trompe*, a horn, trumpet;

tromper, properly to play the horn, alluding to quacks and mountebanks, who attracted the public by blowing a horn, and then cheated them into buying. Brachet].

(5) See Bartlett's *Familiar Quotations*, p. 334, for parallels to Hardcastle's love of old things. **Darby and Joan**, or the Happy Old Couple. A popular ballad, generally said to have been written by Henry Woodfall, a printer and apprentice of John Darby of Bartholomew Close (d. 1730), to whom, and his wife Joan, the ballad refers. The authorship has also been ascribed to Matthew Prior.

(5) **make money of that**, see how much that comes to.

(6) **years of discretion**, full age; the age at which he becomes legally entitled to manage his own affairs; when he attains his majority. Tony, being "under age," was a minor, and his property was controlled by his stepfather.

(7) **nor ever will** (arrive at years of discretion). Hardcastle means he will never be discreet, sensible.

(10) **quotha**, now used as an interjection of contempt, = forsooth, but orig. a corruption of 'quoth I' or 'quoth he.' Ogilvie. [A.-S. *cwethan*, past tense singular, 1. *cwaed*, 2. *cwaede*, 3. *cwaed*, later *quod* = quoth. Possibly, as *quotha* is often apparently a second person, it may also stand for A.-S. *cwaede thû*, quoth thou; at least it

would seem to have been often so understood in old times, whether rightly or wrongly].

(12) **allow him a horsepond,** allow him to be ducked in a horse-pond. If (playing such pranks as) **burning. but,** adv. = only. **fastened my wig** : "an incident which was but the counterpart of a trick played on [Goldsmith] himself during his last visit at Gosfield by the daughter of Lord Clare, which she often related to her son, Lord Nugent." Forster, p. 411.

(13) **a year or two's Latin,** studying Latin for a year or two.

(14) **a cat and a fiddle,** an exclamation like "fiddlestick" = nonsense.

(15) **snub,** thwart, check, reprimand. **consumptive,** affected with or having a tendency to consumption, a wasting disease which most commonly attacks the lungs.

(20) **a speaking-trumpet,** a trumpet-shaped instrument for enabling a person to speak very loudly.

(21) **and I,** Mrs. Hardcastle's grammar is defective.

(23) **raw,** chilly, cold and damp. **look most shockingly,** appear very ill. Tony, as represented by Quick, was the very picture of ruddy health, which made his mother's apprehensions very comic.

(24) **expects,** singular, because *Three Pigeons* is a singular term as the name of an inn. **forward,** on.

(26) **paltry,** lit. ragged, thence vile, mean, worthless.

(27) **Aminadab that grinds the music-box,** some Jewish vagabond musician who played a barrel-organ or a hurdy-gurdy. **that spins the pewter platter,** he used to keep a pewter plate spinning on the table while he sang. Compare G.'s *Essays*, No. I.; another (of the choice spirits) "sung to a plate which he kept trundling on the edges."

(34) **goes . . pair . . spoil: pair** is regarded as a collective noun, and so takes a singular verb, but the relative **that** has a distributive force with **each other,** and so takes the plural **spoil,** in spite of the rule that the relative agrees with its antecedent in number.

(34) **by living** = by having lived. **French frippery,** French fashions and finery, much imitated by the English at all times [*frippery,* worn-out clothes, trifles, O. French *friperie,* a broker's shop for old clothes, &c., cf. Shak. *Tempest,* iv. 225].

(35) **trimmings,** superfluities. **the vain,** vain persons. When an adj. is converted into a noun by prefixing *the,* if it is an abstract noun, as 'the sublime,' it is singular; if a concrete noun, as 'the rich,' it is plural.

(36) **housewife's dress,** housekeeper's dress, of a plain and homely style and material.

(40) **It's** = the chance is = the chances are, a thousand to one.

(41) **pitched upon,** selected.

(50) Perhaps an allusion to Hoadly's play of *The Suspicious Husband,* 1747.

(51) **struck me,** when he was described.

(53) **more than an even wager,** *i.e.* the odds or chances are that he may not have you.

(54) **set my cap,** arrange my head-dress according to some newer fashion. See Wright's *Caricature History of the Georges,* p. 256; Planché's *British Costume,* p. 354.

(55) **the first day's muster,** an adverbial phrase, the so-called "accusative of time," or adverbial objective construction.

(56) **sheepish,** bashful.

(57) **whimsical,** strange, unusual. **in face,** looking well.

(58) **canary birds,** introduced into Europe about 400 years ago from the Canary Isles. **gold-fishes,** bright-coloured fish, brought from China, and often kept in large

glass globes or bowls. **the cat.** See Gray's *Lines on a favourite cat, drowned in a tub of Goldfishes,* in Palgrave's *Golden Treasury,* cxx.

(67) **you own affair,** your love affair with Hastings.

(68) **tête-à-têtes,** conferences [French = *head to head,* thence private, confidential conference]. **pink of perfection,** the acme of excellence. [Mr. Skeat thinks the phrase is probably due to Shakspere's "pink of courtesy," *Rom. and Jul.* ii. iv. 62. *Pink* is a flower of the genus Dianthus, and the name seems to have been given from some of the species being marked with small dots like eyes, *i.e. pinks,* from a verb *pink* = wink. Ogilvie. The pink was a favourite flower in Elizabeth's reign: see Bacon's Essay *Of Gardens,* and so *the pink of courtesy* may have been

a slang phrase, like the modern slang "go it, my tulip," &c.]

(69) **let it go out of the family,** as it would do if she were to marry anyone not belonging to the family.

(70) **too hard,** for her to manage or control. **never once,** never at any time; pleonastic for sake of emphasis.

(71) **holds out,** resists, refuses to marry Constance.

(72) **It,** sometimes used for *he* or *she* before *is;* cf. Shak. *Antony,* iii. ii. 6: "'t is a noble Lepidus." **at bottom,** at heart, substantially. **the improvements.** See Miss Austen's *Mansfield Park,* ch. vi. **Allons!** let us go [Fr.].

(73) **Would it were bedtime,** &c. Sir John Falstaff says: "I would 'twere bedtime, Hal, and all well," *1 Henry IV.* v. i. 125. = I wish it were all over, decided.

ACT I.—Scene 2.

Stage direction: **punch.** Hindustani, *panch,* five: because containing five ingredients, viz., spirit, hot water, lemon peel or juice, sugar, and spices. **a mallet,** a small hammer, generally made of ivory, with which the chairman tapped the table for silence when a toast was to be proposed or a song sung.

(1) **Omnes,** all [Lat.]. **knock himself down,** use the mallet as a signal for silence during his song. See Goldsmith, *Essays,* No. 1.

(4) **genus,** genius: makes the intellect keener. **Their Lethes, their Styxes, and Stygians,** "Lethe, the river of oblivion" (Milton, *Par. Lost,* ii. 583); Styx, the "Stygian flood" (*Par. Lost,* i. 239), " Abhorred Styx, the flood of deadly hate" (*Par. Lost,* ii. 577). [Greek, λήθη = forgetfulness; "but no river is called Λήθη by the ancients." " Στύξ, the Styx, *i.e.* the Hateful ; a river of the nether world, by which the gods in Homer swore their most sacred oaths."

Liddell and Scott. L. and S. may be right about the Greek authors, but Lucan (bk. ix. 355) and Silius Italicus (*Bel. Pun.* i. 235), both Latin writers, seem to speak of a river Lethe.] Goldsmith here seems to imitate Swift's poem on *Hamilton's Bawn.* "The Captain" says:—

"A scholard, when just from his college broke loose,
Can hardly tell how to cry bo to a goose;
Your *Noveds,* and *Bluturcks,* and *Omurs,* and stuff,
By ——, they don't signify this pinch of snuff."

(Noveds, &c. = Ovids, Plutarchs, and Homers). **Their Qui-s,** not *Quis. qui, quæ, quod,* Lat. relative pronoun. **Methodist.** The Methodists in those days excited as much ridicule as the "Salvation Army" people do now, but they did a great deal of good. See Bright's *History of England,* p. 1016; George Eliot's *Silas Marner.* [There was an ancient sect of this name; but the modern Methodists were so called from the fact that the name was applied to John Wesley and his companions by their fellow-students at Oxford, on account of the exact regularity of their lives, and the strictness of their observance of their religious duties. Ogilvie.] **a crown**, five shillings. **a skinful**, when their skin is full of liquor; when they've had plenty to drink. **slice**, portion, helping. **scurvy**, mean, contemptible. **the pigeon**, a slang name for a young man stripped of his money, "plucked," plundered, by gamblers, "hawks." **jorum**, punchbowl. [Perhaps a corruption of *Jordan*, *i.e.* orig. a Jordan-bottle, in which pilgrims brought home water from the holy river Jordan in Palestine. Ogilvie.] **hare**, is a *game* animal, but hardly one of the "gay birds of the air," as the rhyme would require us to believe.

(5) **Bravo**, well done; an Italian exclamation, introduced probably with the Italian opera. Goldsmith makes these vulgar fellows affect "sentimental" opinions, to ridicule those who pronounced his first play low.

(6) **spunk**, lit. fire; spirit, courage.

(9) **concatenation**, a big word which the "Fourth fellow" does not know the meaning of, but is proud to use.

(10) **maxum**, he means "moral" or "sentiment" probably; cf. *Good-Natured Man*, iii. 13. **May this be my poison**, referring to the liquor in his glass. A vulgarism; cf. Goldsmith, *Essays*, No. 6; "may this glass suffocate me," *Citizen of the World*, xxix.; *Vicar of Wakefield*, vii. **tunes**: these were two fashionable airs. **minuet**, here, dance music; a minuet, a slow, graceful dance. [Fr. *menuet*, Lat. *minutus*, small, from the short steps of the dance.]

(11) **come to his own**, succeeded to his property or inheritance.

(12) **choice of**, *of* superfluous.

(13) **takes after**, resembles; cf. *Good-Natured Man*, ii. 44. **winding**, blowing. [From *wind*, air, comes *to wind*, confused with *wind*, to coil. The true past tense is *winded*=blew; but Scott and others have "*wound* his horn."]

(14) **no bastard**, I'll be worthy of my father, like him. **about**, adv.=round.

(15) **a post-chaise**, a hired carriage for conveying travellers from one *post* or stage to another.

(17) **woundily**, a meaningless oath, once common [derived from *woundy*=excessive, an adj. from *wounds*, a profane exclamation, sometimes *His wounds*, or *Zounds*; now obsolete].

(18) **a twinkling**, a winking or twinkling of an eye. **squeezing of a lemon**, see above, Note 10; cf. "My Lord Mudler, one of the most good-natured creatures that ever squeezed a lemon (to make punch)," *Citizen of the World*, liii.

(19) **Father-in-law**, rather stepfather. Southey, *Life of Nelson*, similarly calls Nesbit Nelson's "son-in-law" for "stepson." **grumbletonian**, grumbler, faultfinder, a slang word.

(21) **reserve**, bashfulness, shyness.

(24) **no offence**, an apology for addressing them: I mean no offence by addressing you. We now say, "I beg your pardon," when addressing a total stranger without introduction.

(29) **no ghost, no supernatural** means. We know that already.

(30) **so as**, *so* superfluous.

(32) **whimsical**, Tony's pronunciation of whimsical.

(34) **trapesing**, **trolloping** [*Traipsing* or *Trapesing*, gadding about in a slatternly way, from *trapes*, *traipse*, to walk carelessly (Ogilvie). *Trapes* is still a provincial term for a slattern (Halliwell, *Archaic Dict.*). *Trollop*, related to *trull*, has the same meaning as

Trapes. Ogilvie]. **Maypole**, see Daniel, *Merrie England in the Olden Time*, p. 10. Stubbes, a Puritan writer, in his *Anatomie of Abuses*, 1583 (p. 149, ed. Furnivall, New Sh. Soc.):—"They have twentie or fortie yoke of oxen, euery oxe hauing a sweete nose-gay of flowers placed on the tip of his hornes; and these oxen draw home this Maypole (this stinking Ydol, rather) which is couered all ouer with floures and hearbs, bound round about with strings from the top to the bottome, and sometime painted with variable colours, with two or three hundred men, women, and children, following it with great deuotion. And thus being reared up with handkercheefs and flags houering on the top, they straw the ground round about, binde green boughes about it, set up sommer haules, bowers, and arbors hard by it; and then they fall to daunce about it," &c.

(35) **booby**, loutish, stupid fellow. [Spanish *bobo*, Ital. *balbo*, Lat. *balbus*, a stammerer. Diez, *Etym. Wört.* p. 108, vol. ii.].

apron-string. Children keep dangling about their mothers, and pulling their aprons; hence the saying.

(39) **lock-a-daisy**, a corruption of the old interjection *alack a day*. These directions remind one of Lancelot Gobbo's "Turn up on your right hand at the next turning, but, at the very next turning of all, on your left; marry, at the very next turning, turn of no hand, but turn down indirectly to the Jew's house." *Merchant of Venice*, ii. ii. 42.

(50) **hit it**, found out a way; hit on a plan.

(52) **your**, used "to appropriate an object to a person addressed." See Abbott, *Shakesp. Grammar*, § 221.

(56) **mum**, see note on *Good-Natured Man*, v. 108.

(58) **saving your presence**, ironically, mocking the "landlord;" =by your leave, if you please.

(59) **blade**, slang for fellow. **a**, vulgarism for *he*. Oliphant, *Old and Middle English*, p. 453.

ACT II.

Speech (1) **table exercise**, behaviour during dinner.

(3) **rabbits**, very timid animals. **warren**, ground where rabbits are kept, and where they burrow in great numbers [M.E. *wareine*, from O.F. *warenne*, from Low Lat. *warenna*, from O.H.Ger. *warjan*, to protect. Skeat.]

(8) **yeating**, provincial for *eating*.

(9) **stay**, check.

(10) **stay**, relieve.

(11) This story has not been traced. Apparently it was some anecdote of an old dog named **Grouse** (a favourite name for sporting-dogs), in a **gun-room**, or room in a country house where the guns were kept. "Do we not owe an eternal debt of gratitude to honest Diggory for telling us about ould Grouse in the gun-room, that immortal joke at which thousands and thousands of people have roared with laughter, though they never any one of them could tell what the story was about?" W. Black, *Goldsmith*, p. 144.

(20) **numskulls**, blockheads. **quarrelling for places**, an allusion to the party conflicts in politics at the time.

(21) **by the elevens**, possibly may mean "by the eleven apostles."

(24) **I s'**, provincial for *I shall*, generally written I'ze or ize.

(27) **good housekeeping**, expensive living.

(28) **inflame a reckoning**, add to the bill; cf. *Two Noble Kinsmen*, iii. 5, 127:

> "mine Host
> And his fat Spouse, that welcomes to their cost
> The galled traveller, and with a beckoning
> Informes the tapster to inflame the reckoning;"

(where *tapster* probably retains the feminine force of *-ster*,=barmaid.)

(29) **fleeced**, cheated, charged high, and yet *starved*.

(31) **the Englishman's malady,** awkward reserve.

(32) **of all conscience,** indeed.

(33) **of us,** like men, devoid of the distinctive attribute of their sex, modesty.

(35) **break the ice,** overcome the formality of an interview. **rattle,** talk gaily; cf. below, iii. 124.

(37) **them,** women of reputation. **They may talk,** people may talk. **They,** indef. pron. **bagatelle,** a trifle [Fr.].

(39) **proxy,** deputy [*proxy*, a vulgar contraction of *procuracy, i.e.,* agency, not agent. Similarly *proctor* for *procurator*. Skeat]. **a strain,** an effort.

(41) **my father's** (face).

(43) **inducement down,** an instance of an adverb qualifying a noun=what chiefly induced me to come down here: *down* from town; *up* to town. **honour,** your honourable intentions.

(45) **prepossessing,** though ordinarily meaning inviting favour, attractive, here seems to mean inviting disfavour, prejudicial. *dubeprocessed,* a cant term for bad characters.

(48) Said because Marlow speaks of changing his dress: **use no ceremony,** do not be particular about your dress.

(49) **white and gold,** suit of white, with gold embroidery.

(52) **to besiege Denain.** Denain, in French Flanders, is memorable for the defeat which Marshal Villars there inflicted in 1718 on Prince Eugene. Dyer, *Mod. Eur.* iii. 203. This anecdote of its capture by Marlborough is of course fictitious.

(53) **ventre d'or,** with gold-embroidered front.

(58) **pawn,** wager, stake, pledge.

(62) **a cup,** a mixture of wine and spices, as claret-cup, champagne-cup.

(64) **tolerable,** = satisfactory. **pledge me,** drink a health with me.

(65) **a character,** oddity, humorist.

(67) **warm work,** much business, alluding to his supposed trade. Hardcastle supposes that he means much electioneering work, canvassing, &c. His quotation, "us that sell ale," from some popular song apparently, means "us that give ale for votes;" though the others take it literally as referring to his trade.

(70) **Hyder Ally or Ally Cawn.** Indian questions excited great interest in England about 1773, when Lord North's India Bill was passed. See Taylor's *Hist. of India*, bk. v. ch. xix. ; for *Hyder Ali*, Wheeler's *Short Hist. of India*, p. 316; *Ali Khan* may mean Aliverdy Khan, or Nizam Ali Khan, or Hyder Ali Khan, or Ibrahim Ali Khan, *Khan* being a mere title. **Ally Croaker,** name of an old song.

(72) **half the differences,** half the quarrels of the people of the parish are made up here. Old Hardcastle, as the squire, and a justice of the peace, would often be asked to arbitrate in disputes.

(73) **Westminster Hall,** where the English law-courts were.

(76) **with this** (liquor).

(77) **Belgrade.** Belgrade in Servia, where Prince Eugene defeated a much superior Turkish force, 16th August, 1717. Belgrade capitulated on the 18th. Dyer, *Mod. Eur.* iii. 303.

(81) **brazen dog,** impudent fellow. **these kind,** this kind.

(83) **by the bye,** "the first *by* is a preposition; the second *bye* means 'a town,' 'a particular locality,' found in the suffix *-by*, as in *Derby;* also in the phrase, *bye-law*, or local law, and *byword*, *i.e. town's talk*. The phrase therefore means, 'whilst passing by this place,' tantamount to saying, 'digressing from the general subject,' *this particular topic* (τόπος=place) suggests a similar idea." Fleming, *Anal. Eng. Lang.* p. 118.

(84) **privy council,** private body of councillors; a name strictly used to describe the select council of the sovereign.

(86) **larder,** store-room, where food was kept.

(89) **the high rope,** all his talk about great people.

(90) **Joiners' Company,** one of the trade guilds of the city of London, famous for their love of good cheer. **the corporation of Bedford,** the municipal council of Bedford. Goldsmith had friends in Bedfordshire whom he used to visit; and perhaps while there he heard some stories of the Corporation of Bedford which led to his introducing them here.

(97) **knocked out,** omitted. See note on **your,** i. ii. 52.

(100) **Florentine.** "When any kind of butcher-meat, fowls, apples, &c., are baken in a dish, it is called a *florentine*, and when in a raised crust, a pie." q. Ogilvie. **a shaking pudding,** a jelly. **taffety cream,** or taffeta cream, a dish of thickened cream, which had a smooth or glossy appearance like *taffeta*, *i.e.*, silk. [Fr. *taffetas*, Ital. *taffetà*, Persian *táftah*, woven silk.]

(101) **made dishes,** *entrées*, elaborately prepared food, as distinguished from *plain dishes*, in which the food is plainly cooked. **green and yellow,** where everything is covered with different coloured sauces, so that one does not know what one is eating. English cookery was very simple as compared with French, which consisted chiefly of *made dishes*. **I'm for,** in favour of. **eating,** food.

(103) **aired,** properly dried; a necessary precaution at inns in a damp climate like that of England.

(107) **a very, &c.** Ellipsis for: a very troublesome fellow this; [as troublesome] as I ever met with.

(108) **attend,** wait upon, accompany.

(109) **him,** pronoun referring to *who*.

(114) **hopeful,** mischievous; as in "young hopeful."

(116) **conquest,** has wooed me for him successfully, has made me fall in love with him.

(117) **in France, where even among slaves the laws of marriage are respected.** "'Il a fait,' said Paoli of Goldsmith, 'un compliment très gracieux à une certaine grande dame' [he has paid a very graceful compliment to a certain lady of rank]. The allusion was to a strong intimation in *She Stoops to Conquer* of its author's dislike of the Royal Marriage Act, and sympathy with its victim, the Duchess of Gloucester. The Duke of Cumberland had been forbidden the court on his marriage with a handsome widow, Mrs. Horton (Lord Carhampton's, better known as Colonel Luttrell's, sister), a year before; but on the Duke of Gloucester's subsequent avowal of his marriage with another and more charming widow, Lady Waldegrave (Sir Edward Walpole's natural daughter), the king's indignation found vent in the Royal Marriage Act [1772]; which was hotly opposed by the Whigs as an edict of tyranny, Lords Rockingham and Camden contesting it at every stage in the Lords, and Goldsmith (perhaps for Burke's sake) helping to make it unpopular with the people. 'We'll go to France,' says Hastings

to Miss Neville, 'where even among slaves the laws of marriage are respected.' Said on the first night, this had directed repeated cheering and popular applause to the Duke of Gloucester, who sat in one of the boxes; and it now drew forth the allusion of Paoli." Forster, p. 425. And see Boswell, *Life of Johnson*, vol. i. p. 461 (ed. P. Fitzgerald); Bright's *Hist. England*, p. 1064.

(118) **India director,** one of the directors of the East India Company, most of whom made large fortunes.

(119) **Perish,** imperat. 3rd pers. nom. **baubles,** let the worthless things perish. **let into,** informed of, let into the knowledge of his mistake.

(121) **run the gauntlet.** cf. *The Bee,* No. iv., "obliged to run the *gantelope* through Paternoster-row." [Formerly written *gantlope,* but corrupted to *gantlet* or *gauntlet* by confusion with *gauntlet,* a glove. . . . Again, the *n* is inserted, being no part of the orig. word, which should be *gatlope,* from Swed. *gatlopp,* lit. 'a running down a lane,' because the offender had to run between two files of soldiers, who strike him as he passes; from Swed. *gata,* a street, and *lopp,* a course, career. Skeat.]

(128) **ceremony,** formality, as in "stand upon ceremony."

(130) **Cicero,** Marcus Tullius Cicero, Roman philosopher, orator, and statesman, B.C. 106–43.

(140) **down,** confused; metaphor from boxing or wrestling, = thrown down.

(141) **were,** indicative, past tense, 2nd pers. plur., agr. with **you,** although *you* should be dative case after the adj. **like.** But probably we should take **like** = *such as,* and **you** as in the nom. case in apposition to **observer,** 3rd pers. (Note that nouns in apposition need only agree in *case.*) Or we might take *were* as

subjunctive agreeing with *observer,* but this would make the tense wrong.

(147) **them,** the ladies.

(151) **tastes,** characters; literally, likings, personal inclinations. **some** [persons] **who.**

(160) She is here satirizing his pretended modesty; "rallying" him.

(166) **entertained,** a rather doubtful compliment, which may mean: amused at his confusion, or pleased with his remarks.

(170) **somebody that I know of,** *i.e.* herself; because if she taught him confidence he would make love to her.

(171) **engaging,** assiduous, persistent in engaging my attention.

(173) **it won't do; do** = succeed, a different word from *do* = make. [provin. Eng. *dow,* to avail, be worth, suit; M. E. *duzen,* A.-S. *dugan,* to be worth. Perhaps the phrase 'how do you *do*' is a translation of the O. French 'comment le *faites* vos?' Skeat]. **coquetting,** flirting with him. [From French *coq,* a cock, came the dimin. *coquet,* a little cock, whence the verb *coqueter,* to strut like a cock; the masculine *coquet,* a swaggering beau; fem. *coquette,* a woman who over-exerts herself to gain admiration. Littré. Ogilvie derives Fr. *coquet* from *coqueter;* inverting the true derivation.]

(175) **Ranelagh Gardens,** a popular resort at that time, but of rather bad character. **St. James's,** a fashionable district in London where all the best clubs were. **Tower Wharf,** a district near the Tower of London, inhabited then chiefly by fishwomen, thieves, and vagabonds of all sorts. Hastings is playing on her simplicity.

(176) **only pleased,** you only say it out of politeness; your compliments are only spoken out of kindness. **The Pantheon,** in Spa Fields, near Islington, and Finch's

Grotto Gardens, in St. George's Fields, were two notorious places of entertainment. The following description of the Pantheon, from the *St. James's Chronicle* for 7th May, 1772, will give some idea of these places which Mrs. Hardcastle supposed to be the acme of fashionable life:—"Sir, happening to dine last Sunday with a friend in the city, after coming from church, the weather being very inviting, we took a walk as far as Islington. In our return home towards Cold Bath Fields, we stepped in to view the Pantheon there; but such a scene of disorder, riot, and confusion presented itself to me on my entrance, that I was just turning on my heel in order to quit it, when my friend observing that we might as well have something for our money (for the doorkeeper obliged each of us to deposit a tester [6d.] before he granted us admittance), I acquiesced in his proposal, and became one of the giddy multitude. I soon, however, repented of my choice; for, besides having our sides almost squeezed together, we were in danger every minute of being scalded by the boiling water which the officious Mercuries were circulating with the utmost expedition through their respective districts. We therefore began to look out for some place to sit down in, which with the greatest difficulty we at length procured, and producing our tickets, were served with twelve-pennyworth of punch. Being seated towards the front of one of the galleries, I had now a better opportunity of viewing this dissipated scene. The male part of the company seemed to consist chiefly of city apprentices and the lower class of tradesmen. The ladies, who constituted by far the greater part of the assemblage, seemed mostly to be. . . . Of all the teahouses in the environs of London, the most exceptionable that I have occasion to be in is the Pantheon," quoted by G. Daniel, *Merrie England*, p. 28. **The Borough** is on the Surrey side of London Bridge, and contained several theatres and similar places of amusement. Southwark Fair, a scene of great dissipation, was annually held there.

(177) **dégagée**, free, natural, unconstrained. [Fr.] **friseur**, hairdresser. [Fr. Littré and Brachet say deriv. uncertain; Skeat connects Eng. *frizz*, O. F. *frizer*, with *frieze*, because *frizzled* hair resembles coarse nap of cloth.]

(178) **protest**, declare.

(179) Another ambiguous compliment.

(180) **inoculation**, here *not used* in its modern sense of *vaccination*, which Jenner (1749–1823) did not discover until much after this time, but to a method of causing the disease of small-pox in a mild form by introducing some of the contagious matter beneath the skin of a healthy person. Hence the name **inoculation**, or ingrafting [Lat. *in*, into, *oculus*, an eye, a graft or bud]. "The characteristic of the disease thus induced is its mildness. It protects from small-pox in the same degree as first attacks of that disease protect from second attacks. The objections to it are, (1) that small-pox so induced is infectious; and (2) that it is sometimes fatal." Quain, *Dict. Medicine*, p. 1442. This practice was introduced from Turkey, in the early part of the 18th century. Our older poets make frequent references to the ravages of small-pox, which was for nearly two centuries the scourge of Europe, see Dryden, p. 333, Globe ed.; Pope, p. 243, Globe ed. Since the spread of *vaccination* the virulence and prevalence of small-pox have decreased steadily and rapidly, and the older *inoculation* is now pro-

hibited by law in England. **plain woman**, ugly; here disfigured by pock-marks. **escape** (notice) **in the crowd** (of beauties).

(182) **dressing**, *sc.* fashionably. **argue down**, persuade him to wear clothes of modern style.

(184) **Gothic**, barbarous, unpolished, uncivilized. **tête**, headdress. [Fr. *tête*, O. F. *teste*, Lat. *testa*, the skull. Brachet. See *testa* in Smith's *Lat. Dict.*] An ode to the ladies in 1768, quoted in Wright's *Caricature History*, p. 254, describes the lover's surprise :—

"When he views your tresses thin
Tortured by some French friseur;
Horsehair, hemp, and wool within,
Garnished with a diamond skewer.

When he scents the mingled steam
Which your plastered heads are rich in,
Lard, and meal, and clouted cream,
Can he love a walking kitchen?"

(185) **become**, suit.

(189) **samplers**, patterns in needlework. See Shak. *Mids. N. Dream*, iii. ii. 205. [A form of *exemplar*, O. F. *examplaire* or *examplaire*, Lat. *exemplar*. Skeat.] **Mrs. Niece**, read *Mistress* Niece; ironical=my niece is such a fine lady that, &c. [The form Miss, a contraction of Mistress, as a title of unmarried girls, did not become common until the reign of George III., though it was occasionally used even so early as the Restoration, at first in a bad sense. See Skeat, *Etym. Dict.*]

(191) **niece**, said with great astonishment, as if he took them to be sisters.

(192) **contracted**, betrothed.

(196) **crack**, a cant term for a lie.

(197) His mouth resembles the mouths of her family, the Blenkinsops. **to a T**, exactly. ["The allusion is to a mechanic's T-square, by which accuracy in making angles is secured." Ogilvie.] **of a sign**, the same height.

(201) **a man**, of age, no longer

a minor or 'infant.' **no longer**, vulgarism for *any* longer.

(202) **work**, embroider. **receipt**, recipe, prescription. [*Receipt*, the act or acknowledgment of receiving something; *recipe*, a doctor's prescription, from the first word, Lat. *recipe* = take. These words are often confused, as here.]

(203) **coursing**, giving me a course of the treatment recommended by Dr. Quincy.

(205) **dinging it**, beating, hammering it; also pronounced *dinning it*, as if from a verb *to din;* but the true verb is *ding*, past t. *dung* or *dinged*, p. p. same, though the form *to din* is found as early as the 17th century. Ogilvie gives both verbs. [The A.-S. *dencgan*, quoted by Ogilvie, is said by Mr. Skeat to be probably an invention of Somner's, but he thinks the verb to be of Eng. origin, rather than Scandinavian, as the Eng. verb is strong, the cognate Scand. verbs are weak. Mr. Oliphant, *Old and Middle Eng.* p. 365, calls it a Danish word, from Icelandic *dengia*, to hammer.]

(206) **kennel**, where the hounds were kept. [O. Fr. from Lat. *canis*, a dog; not to be confused with *kennel* = channel, canal.]

(215) **cantackerous**, for 'cantankerous' [prefix *con*, and O. F. *tanser*, *tancer*, to chide or reprimand. Ogilvie. See Diez, *Etym. Wirt.* ii. 438] **toad**, vulgarly supposed to be venomous. See Shaksp. *Lucrece*, 850; *As You Like It*, ii. i. 13; *Richard II.* iii. ii. 15, &c.

(217) **of that**, holding out his hand to show the height. **breaking**, training.

(219) **as loud**, as noisy as a pig caught in the bars of a gate.

(221) **curb . . kick . . flung**. Tony's conversation is naturally *horsy*.

(223) **Bandbox**, a box for ribbons, bonnets, &c. Here = artificial, made up. **mun**, provincial

for *man*. **of these parts,** from this part of the country. **pulpit cushion,** a red cushion was often placed on the pulpit of a church to serve as a support for the parson's book. **two of she,** of her. Tony prefers a big *bouncing* woman; Bet **Bouncer** is well named.

(225) **Anon** = again, say that again=what? a provincialism.

(228) **whip,** carry quickly.

(229) **trundle,** roll, wheel.

ACT III.

Speech (1) **easy-chair,** Mr. H.'s own special arm-chair.

(3) **observe,** follow.

(8) **masquerade,** fancy ball. See the *Spectator*, Nos. 8 and 14, and Prof. Morley's note.

(13) **mauvaise honte,** bashfulness, awkward shyness. [French.]

(16) **Bully Dawson:** "a noted London sharper, who swaggered and led a most abandoned life about Blackfriars, in the reign of Charles II." Brewer. Not to be confused with Jemmy Dawson, the hero of a ballad in Percy's *Reliques*. **to** = in comparison to.

(20) **pun.** [The older sense of to *pun* is to pound=to beat; hence **to pun** is to pound words, to beat them into new senses, to hammer at forced similes. Skeat. This meaning of the word does not seem to be older than the Restoration. To the examples in Skeat add, Farquhar, *Love and a Bottle*, ii. 2: "how it *puns* and quibbles in the glass."]

(26) **done my business,** sufficed for me.

(28) **furniture,** qualities.

(30) **Mr. Brazen,** Mr. Impudence.

(34) **bobs,** ear ornaments. "In jewels dressed and at each ear a bob." Dryden. [Lit. tassel, cluster; of Keltic origin.] **genus,** genius, as above I. ii. 4.

(36) **bear your charges,** defray your expenses.

(38) **fibs,** a euphemism for *lies*. **rule of thumb,** practical experience. **bureau,** cabinet [French, *bureau*, from *bure*, coarse woollen cloth, thence a table covered with bureau or baize; a desk or cabinet. Low Lat. *burra*. Brachet].

(42) **the bounce of a cracker;** an adverbial phrase=as much as the recoil of a cracker or firework. **Morrice, prance!** The cry of the hobby-horse rider in the Morrice or Moorish dances (at May games), which survived in rural districts down to the end of the 18th century. See Strutt, *Sports and Pastimes*, bk. III. chap. v. xviii. p. 223, ed. 1831.

(45) **out,** out of fashion. **bring nothing but paste and marcasites back,** because they lose their jewels at cards. **paste,** "a highly refractive variety of glass, a composition of pounded rock-crystal melted with alkaline salts, and coloured with metallic oxides; used for making imitation gems." **Marcasite** [a word of Arabic origin], "Iron pyrites or bisulphide of iron." Ogilvie.

(46) **somebody,** Hastings; not Tony, as Mrs. Hardcastle supposes.

(48) **That's as thereafter may be** = that depends (on circumstances).

(50) **rose-cut,** "a term applied to gems, the back of which is left flat, and the face cut into a series of inclined triangular facets arranged round a central hexagon." Ogilvie. **table-cut,** a gem whose upper surface is flat, the sides being angular. **King Solomon,** see Goldsmith's *Essays*, No. VI. Scenes from the Bible, such as the court of Solomon, the vow of Jephthah, Daniel in the lion's den, &c., were often exhibited in puppet-shows at fairs.

(51) **witness**, here used in its original sense of evidence, an abstract noun, like thick*ness*, blind*ness*, &c.

(61) **garnets** [*garnet*, older form *granat*, through French from Latin *granatus*, either because of "its resemblance in colour and shape to the grains of the pomegranate"—Webster, q. Skeat—or, as Ogilvie says, from Lat. *granum*, grain, seed; the cochineal insect and the dye obtained from it—cochineal insects being once supposed to be the seeds of a species of oak].

(64) **trumpery**, worthless finery.

(67) **Catharine wheel**, a kind of firework, "supposed to represent the wheel upon which St. Catharine suffered martyrdom" (Cussans' *Handbook of Heraldry*, p. 113).

(77) **make me for to laugh**, a provincialism for make me laugh.

(80) **cross-grained**, obstinate, perverse; from timber, which is hardest to cut across the *grain* or lie of the fibres.

(86) **that brother of mine.** See Notes on *Good-Natured Man.* **his** (Marlow's) **impudence.**

(88) **Cherry**, the daughter of the Landlord Boniface, in Farquhar's best play, *The Beaux' Stratagem.* Cherry (I. i.) says: "Chamberlain, show the Lion and the Rose"—apartments so named, as are "the Lamb," "the Angel," &c.

(96) Miss Hardcastle quotes from *The Good-Natured Man*, act v. sp. 9. **bar cant**, way of speaking common among barmaids.

(98) **host**, landlord.

(104) **tablets**, memorandum-book.

(112) **nectar**, honeyed sweetness; lit. the drink of the gods, in Greek mythology, as ambrosia was their food.

(113) **no French wines**, an instance of the feeling also displayed in Mr. Flanagan's indignation against the "parlez-voos," *Good-Natured Man*, act iii.

(119) A horse's age can be known by certain marks on his teeth.

(121) **obstropalous**, obstreperous. **before a justice**; as a prisoner before a judge.

(122) **rallied**, bantered.

(124) **Rattle** = chatterbox.

(126) **Miss Biddy Buckskin**, a real character, and friend of Horace Walpole's. **The club** was the Albemarle Street club. See Forster, p. 419.

(130) **chit**, young thing. [A.S. *cith*, a shoot or sprout.]

(136) **nicked**, scored; **ames ace**, or **amb's ace**, the lowest throw upon the dice, both aces; cf. Shak. *All's Well*, II. iii. 85. [Fr. *ambesas*, O.F. *ambes*, plur. of *ambe*, from Lat. *ambo*, both, and Lat. *as*, ace, unit, a Tarentine form of Greek *heis*, one. Og. and Sk.]

(139) **infectious**; he means that Miss H. is becoming impudent too.

(141) **prerogatives**, rights, privileges (including the easy-chair by the fireside. See act. iv. sp. 60).

(145) **mind**, attend to, understand,

ACT IV.

Speech (2) **depend upon**, trust, believe.

(3) **my name**, a slip on Goldsmith's part. Mrs. Hardcastle addresses him as "Mr. Hastings" several times in act ii.

(5) **elopement**, running away [akin to *lope* in *gantlope*, act ii. sp. 121, note; *elope*, corrupted, by

substitution of the familiar prefix *e-*, from Dutch *ontloopen*, with Romance suffix -*ment*].

(31) **forthcoming**, production.

(32) **with a witness**, ambiguous, may mean "with a vengeance," as Hastings uses it in his disappointment. See Shak. *Taming of the*

Shrew, v. i. 121 ; Farquhar, *Sir Harry Wildair*, i. i. ; iv. ii.

(40) **it**, the casket.

(42) **topsy-turvy**, a contraction of *topside t'other way*.

(47) **make up**, atone, by drinking for "the good of the house," profit of the innkeeper.

(52) **liberty and Fleet-street**, one of the cant cries of the time, in imitation of "Wilkes and liberty," and alluding probably to the riot called the "battle of Templebar." Wright's *Caric. Hist.* p. 315.

(53) **soused**, ducked, dipped.

(62) **Rake's Progress**, a famous series of pictures by William Hogarth (1697 – 1764), showing the gradual ruin of a young man who falls into vicious courses.

(64) **mahogany**: Boswell, *Life of Johnson*, vol. ii. p. 456, makes Johnson say: "*Mahogany* must be a modern name; for it was not long since the wood called mahogany was known in this country." This was on the 30th March, 1781, so we may suppose that Mr. H.'s table, in which you might see your own face (it was so brightly polished), was a new and valuable bit of furniture.

(79) **Dullissimo macaroni**=the most dull Macaroni. "The grand phenomena of the years 1772 and 1773 were the Macaronis. Men of fashion in the earlier part of the reign of George II. had been commonly designated by the appellation of *beaux;* about the year 1749 they began to be termed *fribbles*, a name which continued in use during the first years of the reign of George III. Then a number of young men who had made the tour, and had returned from Italy with all the vices and follies they had picked up there, formed themselves into a club, which, from the dish which peculiarly distinguished their table, they called the *Macaroni Club*. The members of this club soon became distinguished by

the title of *Macaronis;* it was their pride to carry to the utmost excess every description of dissipation, effeminacy of manners, and modish novelty of dress," &c. See Wright's *Caricature Hist. of the Georges*, pp. 258-261, for an illustrated account of them, from which the above is taken.

(81) **subscriber**, adding you to the list. **assurance**, immodesty.

(85) **simplicity**, simple one; abstract for concrete.

(91) **whistlejacket**, perhaps the name of a race-horse. It was a Lincolnshire term for "small beer." Halliwell's *Arch. Dict.*

(92) **fairly**, properly. **billing**, kissing, as pigeons *bill*, touch their bills together, caress each other.

(93) **no love lost between us**, we are not friends. Bartlett, *Famil. Quotations*, p. 347, refers to Garrick's *Correspondence*, 1759; Fielding's *Grub-street Opera*, i. iv.

(94) **sprinkling**, check, as a little water upon fire.

(95) **It**, expressive of fondness, addressing children. See Notes on *Good-Natured Man.*

(96) **pound**, inclosure for stray animals.

(99) **haspicolls**, Tony's way of saying harpsichord, a musical instrument something like a pianoforte, which superseded it about the middle of the eighteenth century.

(99) **bobbins**, long reels of thread, used in spinning.

(100) **incontinently**, immediately. **Like Dr. Drowsy's sermons**, as Dr. D. (the rector of the parish) puts off the rest of his sermon to another Sunday.

(105) **mun**, Scotch *maun*=must. [The Scandinavian verb *muna*, orig. *to will*, as *I mun do this* (*ormulum*, 1200 A.D.) = I will do this ; the meaning *must* (*oportet*) seems to have crept in about 1300. See Oliphant's *Old and Middle English*, pp. 226, 325, 355, &c.]

(108) buzz, confusion. (See *The Slang Dictionary*, p. 105.)

(112) izzard, the old name for the letter *z*.

(116) cut . . . out of feather, surpassed, conquered.

(119) sinister, dishonest, treacherous. [Lat. *sinister*, left, left hand, bad; the Romans derived from the Greeks the notion that the left hand was unlucky. Skeat.]

(120) ill-fashioned oaf, ugly-shaped fool [*oaf*, or *aulf*, Scandinavian form of *elf*]. wish you better, compar. of to wish a person *well;* cf. well-wisher.

(124) making believe, feigning, pretending.

(126) another (come to find fault with me).

(125) my servant. It was Diggory who brought the letter.

(128) old Bedlam, a perfect lunatic asylum. old was formerly used = great, as in Shak. *Much Ado*, v. ii. 98: "yonder's old coil at home;" *Mer. of Venice*, iv. ii. 15: "we shall have old swearing;" *Macb.* ii. iii. 2: "he should have old turning the key." Bedlam = Bethlehem hospital, orig. the hospital of St. Mary of Bethlehem, a lunatic asylum, founded by Henry VIII. in 1547.

(130) age = youth.

(135) Baw or boh (see above, i. ii. 4), rustic exclamation of defiance. with baskets, fencing-sticks, which have guards for the hand made of basket-work.

(139) kept on, kept up.

(140) putting to, being yoked. a gerund, *to* being adverbial = are *a-putting-to*.

(142) an explanation, an apology, the alternative of refusing which would be a challenge to fight a duel.

(156) Sulky, Marlow.

ACT V.— Scene 1.

Speech (18) take = *comprehend*, understand.

(20) mum, silence, say no more about it.

(22) rumpled, romped with.

(24) over-acting, "making-believe" too much.

(54) convinced, that this description of him is untrue.

ACT V.—Scene 2.

Speech (1) booted, in top-boots, riding-boots; spattered, splashed with mud.

(5) rabbit me, confound me [O.F. *rabbatre*, to beat down, to humble. Eng. *rebate*. See Notes on *Good Natured Man*]. varmint, vulgar for *vermin;* bad horses, he means.

(11) by jingo, a mild sort of oath. [Der. uncert. Some say a corruption of *Saint Gengulphus* or *Gingoulf;* others, the Basque *jingo*, god].

(13) crack, straight, adv. circumbendibus, a circuitous way. [A ludicrous compound of Lat. *circum*, round; Eng. *bend*, and Lat. case-ending *-bus* or *-ibus*.]

(15) cattle, horses [Properly 'capital' or 'chattel,' i.e., property, without reference to live stock. The M. E. words *catel* and *chatel* are mere variants of one and the same word, and both mean 'property.' O.Fr. *catel, chatel*, Low Lat. *capitale*, Lat. *capitalis*, from *caput*, head. Skeat]. whip off, ride off, be off, escape.

(17) kiss the hangman, go to the gallows. The criminal sometimes kissed the hangman, as a token of forgiveness.

(19) draggled, wet and muddy.

(20) quick-set, lit. set, planted, with quick, living, shrubs. done my business, done for me, killed me.

(21) **would be for**, insisted on.

(25) **kept**, resorted.

(33) **keep close**, keep hidden.

(51) **graceless**, mischievous; lit. deprived of divine grace, base, wicked.

(52) **varlet**, rogue. Orig. a feudal term for boys from seven to fourteen years of age. "The first of these [four distinct causes tending to the promotion of chivalry] was the regular scheme of education, according to which the sons of gentlemen from the age of seven years were brought up in the castles of superior lords, where they at once learned the whole discipline of their future profession, and imbibed its emulous and enthusiastic spirit. This was an inestimable advantage to the poorer nobility, who could hardly otherwise have given their children the accomplishments of their station. From seven to fourteen these boys were called *varlets* or pages; at fourteen they bore the name of Esquire. They were instructed in the management of arms, in the art of horsemanship, in exercises of strength and activity. They became accustomed to obedience and courteous demeanour, serving their lord or lady in offices which had not yet become derogatory to honourable birth, and striving to please visitors, and especially ladies, at the ball or banquet." Hallam, *Eur. in Middle Ages*, p. 819, one vol. ed. [*Varlet*, older from *vaslet*, dimin. of *vassal*, O. Fr. from Low Lat. *vassallus*, a word of Keltic origin. Eng. *valet* is the mod. French form of *vaslet*. Skeat]. **abuse**, misuse, play tricks on.

(55) **morality**, moral philosophy.

(58) **fortune**, wealth.

ACT V.—Scene 3.

Speech (6) **improves upon me**, rises in my estimation.

(7) **imputed merit**, merit ascribed or attributed to me.

(10) **steals**, causes some new grace to steal in; causative.

(16) **mercenary**, actuated by mean motives.

(27) **keeps it up**, amuses himself, keeps up amusement.

(42) **tenderness**, compassion. **from a nearer connection**, because of, or, for sake of, the claims of kindred.

(49) **these presents**, a law term = these present writings.

(50) **the favour** (by wishing me joy).

EPILOGUE.

Line (8) from Shak. *As You Like It*, ii. vii. 141.

(18) **connoisseurs**, critical judges of good looks [Fr.].

(20) **gridiron**, at the chophouses the barmaid used to cook chops and steaks at a fire in the eating-room. Her lovers watched her while she was broiling chops, and became more enamoured.

(21) **her triumphs to complete**, adverbial to the next line.

(25) **caro**, dear, excellent [Ital.].

(26) = quits her ballads for Italian music.

(27) **doats upon**, is mad about.

(28) **swims**, glides in the dance. **Heinel**, a celebrated dancer.

(31) **spadille**, another name for the game of cards called *ombre*, in which the spadille, spadillio, or ace of spades, was the strongest card. See Pope's *Rape of the Lock*, and the notes thereon.

(32) **Barrister**, a pun on *Bar*maid. **Bays**, either "poetic laurels," or "the poet himself," from *Bayes*, a poet, character in the Duke of Buckingham's play, *The Rehearsal*.

APPENDIX TO THE NOTES.

UNSPOKEN EPILOGUES TO "SHE STOOPS TO CONQUER."

AMONG the difficulties against which the author had to contend was the rivalry of the actresses who were to play the parts of Miss Hardcastle and Miss Neville. Forster says:—"Murphy volunteered an epilogue, but the lady who was not to speak it objected to the lady who was; the author wrote an epilogue to bring in both, and the lady first objected to objected in her turn; a third epilogue was then written by poor Goldsmith, to which Colman himself thought proper to object as being too bad to be spoken; Cradock meanwhile sent a fourth from the country; rejected for a similar reason (but politely printed with the comedy as having arrived 'too late'), and Goldsmith finally tried his hand at a fifth, which, though permitted to be spoken, he thought 'a mawkish thing.'" See Goldsmith's letter to Cradock in Forster, p. 415. Three of these rejected Epilogues are here reprinted :—

AN INTENDED EPILOGUE TO "SHE STOOPS TO CONQUER."

To be spoken in the character of Tony Lumpkin.

BY J. CRADOCK, ESQ.

Well—now all's ended—and my comrades gone,
Pray what becomes of mother's nonly son?
A hopeful blade !—in town I'll fix my station,
And try to make a bluster in the nation;
As for my cousin Neville, I renounce her;
Off, in a crack, I'll carry big Bett Bouncer.
Why should not I in the great world appear?
I soon shall have a thousand pounds a year !
No matter what a man may here inherit,
In London—'gad, they've some regard to spirit.
I see the horses prancing up the streets,
And big Bett Bouncer bobs to all she meets;
Then hoiks to jigs and pastimes every night—
Not to the plays—they say it a'n't polite;
To Sadler's-Wells perhaps, or operas go,
And once by chance to the roratorio.
Thus here and there, for ever up and down,
We'll set the fashions too to half the town;
And then at auctions—money ne'er regard,
Buy pictures, like the great, ten pounds a yard;
Zounds, we shall make these London gentry say,
We know what's damned genteel as well as they.

ANOTHER INTENDED EPILOGUE TO "SHE STOOPS TO CONQUER."

Enter MRS. BULKLEY, *who curtsies very low as beginning to speak. Then enter* MISS CATLEY, *who stands full before her, and curtsies to the Audience.*

Mrs. Bul. Hold, Ma'am, your pardon. What's your business here?
Miss Cat. The Epilogue.
Mrs. Bul. The Epilogue?
Miss Cat. Yes, the Epilogue, my dear.
Mrs. Bul. Sure you mistake, Ma'am. The Epilogue! *I* bring it.
Miss Cat. Excuse me, Ma'am. The Author bid *me* sing it.

RECITATIVE.

Ye beaux and belles, that form this splendid ring,
Suspend your conversation while I sing.

Mrs. Bul. Why, sure the girl's beside herself! an Epilogue of singing!
A hopeful end indeed to such a blest beginning.
Besides, a singer in a comic set!—
Excuse me, Ma'am, I know the etiquette.
Miss Cat. What if we leave it to the House?
Mrs. Bul. The House!—Agreed.
Miss Cat. Agreed.
Mrs. Bul. And she whose party's largest shall proceed.
And first, I hope you'll readily agree
I've all the critics and the wits for me.
They, I am sure, will answer my commands:
Ye candid judging few, hold up your hands.
What! no return? I find too late, I fear,
That modern judges seldom enter here.
Miss Cat. I'm for a different set.—Old men, whose trade is
Still to gallant and dangle with the ladies.

RECITATIVE.

Who mump their passion, and who, grimly smiling,
Still thus address the fair with voice beguiling:

AIR.—*Cotillon.*

Turn, my fairest, turn, if ever
    Strephon caught thy ravished eye.
Pity take on your swain so clever,
    Who without your aid must die.
Yes, I shall die, hu, hu, hu, hu!
Yes, I shall die, ho, ho, ho, ho!
                                    Da capo.

Mrs. Bul. Let all the old pay homage to your merit:
Give me the young, the gay, the men of spirit.
Ye travelled tribe, ye macaroni train,
Of French friseurs and nosegays justly vain,
Who take a trip to Paris once a year
To dress and look like awkward Frenchmen here,
Lend me your hands.—O fatal news to tell!
Their hands are only lent to the Heinel.

Miss Cat.   Ay, take your travellers, travellers indeed!
        Give me my bonny Scot, that travels from the Tweed.
        Where are the chiels?—Ah, ah, I well discern
        The smiling looks of each bewitching bairn.

AIR.—*A bonnie young Lad is my Jockey.*

        I'll sing to amuse you by night and by day,
        And be unco' merry when you are but gay;
        When you with your bagpipes are ready to play,
        My voice shall be ready to carol away
                With Sandy, and Sawney, and Jockey,
                With Sawney, and Jarvie, and Jockey.

Mrs. Bul.   Ye gamesters, who so eager in pursuit
        Make but of all your fortune one *va toute:*
        Ye Jockey tribe, whose stock of words are few;
        "I hold the odds.—Done, done, with you, with you:"
        Ye barristers, so fluent with grimace,
        "My Lord,—your Lordship misconceives the case:"
        Doctors, who cough and answer every misfortuner,
        "I wish I'd been called in a little sooner:"
        Assist my cause with hands and voices hearty;
        Come, end the contest here, and aid my party.

AIR.—*Ballinamony.*

Miss Cat.   Ye brave Irish lads, hark away to the crack,
        Assist me, I pray, in this woful attack;
        For sure I don't wrong you, you seldom are slack,
        When the ladies are calling, to blush and hang back.
                For you're always polite and attentive,
                Still to amuse us inventive,
                And death is your only preventive:
                Your hands and your voices for me.

Mrs. Bul.   Well, Madam, what if, after all this sparring,
        We both agree, like friends, to end our jarring?
Miss Cat.   And that our friendship may remain unbroken,
        What if we leave the Epilogue unspoken?
Mrs. Bul.   Agreed.
Miss Cat.   Agreed.
Mrs. Bul.   And now with late repentance
        Un-epilogued the Poet waits his sentence.
        Condemn the stubborn fool who can't submit
        To thrive by flattery, though he starves by wit.   [*Exeunt.*

A THIRD INTENDED EPILOGUE TO "SHE STOOPS TO CONQUER."

To be spoken by Mrs. Bulkley.

        THERE is a place, so Ariosto sings,
        A treasury for lost and missing things:
        Lost human wits have places there assigned them,
        And they who lose their senses there may find them.
        But where's this place, this storehouse of the age?
        The Moon, says he:—but *I* affirm, the Stage:

At least in many things, I think, I see
His lunar and our mimic world agree.
Both shine at night; for, but at Foote's alone,
We scarce exhibit till the sun goes down:
Both prone to change, no settled limits fix:
And sure the folks of both are lunatics.
But in this parallel my best pretence is,
That mortals visit both to find their senses;
To this strange spot rakes, macaronies, cits,
Come thronging to collect their scattered wits.
The gay coquette, who ogles all the day,
Comes here at night, and goes a prude away.
Hither the affected city dame advancing,
Who sighs for operas, and doats on dancing,
Taught by our art her ridicule to pause on,
Quits the *ballet*, and calls for *Nancy Dawson*.
The gamester, too, whose wit's all high or low,
Oft risks his fortune on one desperate throw,
Comes here to saunter, having made his bets,
Finds his lost senses out, and pays his debts.
The Mohawk too, with angry phrases stored,
As "Dam'me, Sir," and "Sir, I wear a sword,"
Here lessoned for a while, and hence retreating,
Goes out, affronts his man, and takes a beating.
Here come the sons of scandal and of news,
But find no sense—for they had none to lose.
Of all the tribe here wanting an adviser,
Our Author's the least likely to grow wiser;
Has he not seen how you your favour place
On sentimental queens and lords in lace?
Without a star, a coronet, or garter,
How can the piece expect or hope for quarter?
No high-life scenes, no sentiment: the creature
Still stoops among the low to copy nature.
Yes, he's far gone:—and yet some pity fix,
The English laws forbid to punish lunatics.

ADDITIONAL NOTES

Page

86. *Insert note:* (46) the longitude. The question of accurately determin-
ing longitude at sea occupied the attention of men of science during
the eighteenth century, and the offer of a reward by Government led
to "finding out the longitude" becoming a cant phrase for an impos-
sibility. The invention of accurate chronometers solved the difficulty.

88. Note 90, *add:* But Junius (i. 213, Bohn's ed.) tells us that the Duke of
Bedford, "the little tyrant of a little corporation," was "held in such
contempt and detestation, that, in order to deliver themselves from
him, they (the corporation of Bedford) admitted a number of strangers
to the freedom." Hence the *corporation* would be unusually large, and
would include all the *freemen* of the city.